God, Jesus and Life in the Spirit

Bishop Lyttelton
Library
Winchester

David E. Jenkins
Bishop of Durham

God, Jesus and Life in the Spirit

SCM PRESS LTD

© David E. Jenkins 1988

British Library Cataloguing in Publication Data

Jenkins, David E. (David Edward), 1925–
   God, Jesus and life in the spirit.
   1. Christian life
   I. Title
   248.4

ISBN 0–334–02018–2

First published 1988
by SCM Press Ltd
26–30 Tottenham Road, London N1 4BZ

Printed in Great Britain by
Richard Clay Ltd, Bungay, Suffolk

Contents

Preface

This book puts together some attempts of mine to explain what Christian faith is about and why and how the biblical story about God, men and women and the world has a compelling and attracting power to do with life today – and with this life at its deepest and most promising levels. The book starts with three talks which were aimed at explaining to a student audience at London University why I felt compelled to commend this faith and story to them and how the faith and the story were of the greatest worth and importance for all of us in a deeply threatened world.

The group from London University Chaplaincy with whom I planned these talks for delivery in February 1987 worked out the title for the series as 'Cut to the Heart of the Matter'. I understood that by this they were indicating that they wanted me to cut out religious verbiage, evasion and unreality and to 'cut to the heart of the matter' about the possibilities of God and about the possibilities of ourselves in our world. I do not know how far I succeeded but I felt obliged to try. The audience kept up its numbers and spent a good deal of time pressing its questions in a sympathetic, although testing, way which suggested that, at least, we were on a common exploration. I did not see that I could begin on this enterprise and exploration in any other way than by saying something about how I got caught up with, and am kept going on, this way of exploration. The first three chapters, therefore, serve as some sort of partial and unfinished confession of faith.

They are followed by a version of a series of four talks which I repeated at four centres in my diocese during the winter of 1984–85 and 1985. Their purpose was to seize on the widespread interest aroused publically about what I was supposed to believe and not believe as an opportunity to make systematic teaching accessible to anyone from any part of the diocese who wanted it. The object of the series was not to answer controversies but to strengthen faith and extend explorations. Not everything could be covered – although God, Jesus, People and the Holy Spirit and the Church is a fairly comprehensive list of topics! But the object was to show the scope of the Christian faith and story and the liveliness, expansiveness and practicality of its pursuit, rather than to expound or insist on doctrinal tidiness. Hence the informal style of the original delivery has been deliberately kept. I was, and am, offering living insights into the riches and experience of the Christian biblical and doctrinal traditions for a living encounter today with the living God.

After this I have reproduced in the third section of the book the Christmas and Easter sermons which I have preached in Durham Cathedral since I have been Bishop. They are here, first, because of the intrinsic importance of their themes. Incarnation and resurrection are central to the Christian faith, the Christian story and the Christian hope. But they are also included because preaching – expounding, exploring, explaining and proclaiming what one has first received, seen, encountered – is a central part of Christian experience, worship and mission. This is so because within the biblical records and within the life, recruitment and renewal of the Christian church, the categories and experiences of gift, encounter and call are central and preaching is the witness to this.

Christian faith is a Way – of perceiving life, receiving life, practising life and pursuing life. Finding oneself on that Way, or choosing or seeking to go on that Way are very much matters of receiving a gift, coming up against a demand which is also an offer, being engaged by a possibility and a presence which will not let you go, catching glimpses of an enticement or a provocation which must be followed up. It is all to do with God somehow or other focussed by, illuminated through, and pointed to by, Jesus –

the Jesus who is reflected and refracted through the stories, arguments, explorations and hopes which make up the New Testament (against the necessary background of the Old).

But as a precondition of, and necessity for, the very existence of the writings ('scriptures') of the Old and New Testaments, and as an absolutely essential part of the possibility of these scriptures coming alive in relation to a living faith in a living God, there has to be, there has been and there is, the various *'People* of the Way'. These are people who have, in one way or another, received the call, the invitation, the gift, the perception and the enticement to follow, receive, acknowledge, so that, however inadequately, they are concerned to worship the God revealed as the giver of all this and made known through all this. So they are committed to following, finding and extending the Way of living in the world, through the world and for the world, which is offered and commanded by this God 'in the name of Jesus'.

To be or become a Christian, therefore, depends on being caught up with, or being enticed, provoked and aggravated by, the existing active 'People of the Way'. Such people, I am quite clear, are not confined to one particular church, nor can one particular church guarantee that a particular group, or individual, among its membership will believe or behave in a manner consistent with the Way or in a manner which is likely to attract other people to the Way. As I had to point out in my preceding publication of pieces on *God, Politics and the Future*, the People of the Way (which stems from and leads to God 'in the name of Jesus') seem so often to deny the way of Jesus Christ, confuse the way of Jesus Christ and lose the way of Jesus Christ. But this is where the act of preaching and the call to preach come in.

Preaching is the proclamation and sharing of a gift received, a tradition of revelation come alive, a Way opened up. It is therefore at the heart of worship which gathers together the life and faith of the People of the Way, which confronts us with our shortcomings along the way, and enables us to celebrate, not our failures and our faithlessness, but God's faithfulness and restoring promise. So preaching is to do also with deepening faith, renewing faith and extending faith. God's gift and presence is to be shared and allowed to grow because God gives, in and through the worship and the preaching, constant reminders and challenges of his repeated and redeeming givingness. Preaching is also an attempt to reach out beyond the faithful (who always require to be challenged, judged, renewed and expanded in their faith) to listeners and seekers, and the heedless and the lost in the world at large. For God is the giver who wills and wishes to give to all, so that all may share in the enrichment of his giving, not only by receiving but also by giving themselves. So preaching is at the heart of worship, is directed to celebrating and deepening discipleship, and is an invitation, and instrument of mission.

This is why some examples of preaching needed to be included in this book. My immediately preceding books (*God, Miracle and the Church of England* and *God, Politics and the Future*) are offered as finding God in and through problems. This book is meant to be about finding God because God finds us.

I hope it will be obvious, therefore, why it is rounded off by a piece on 'Why Pray?' (originally a university sermon preached at Leeds University on Sunday 13 May 1988) and 'Spiritualities for the End of a Century' which is compiled from the substance of two addresses which I gave to a clergy conference in Norwich diocese several years ago. I got the material out to go into this book because I think it does reflect what I have been struggling to practise and pursue for many years and gives some slight indication of what 'keeps me going'. Whatever the disappointing inadequacies of my response I cannot avoid the claim, and the attempt to make good the claim, that I am responding to the amazing possibilities of God – a share in a sharing which must be shared.

DAVID JENKINS
July 1988

PART ONE

The Heart of the Matter: A Personal Confession of Faith

1

Good God – Any Future?

I shall try to begin at a beginning which is at least recognizable, even if it is not fully acceptable, to everybody. And after reflection this leads me to conclude that I must begin with myself.

Becoming a bishop, especially the way it has happened to me, has called me in question. Before that I pursued a calling and a career which, on the whole, I enjoyed both as a priest and as an academic. I felt myself called to and committed to teaching, preaching and exploring Christianity in all the ways which were open to me: in my teaching, in my dealings with the churches at parish level and in meeting with people in connection with all sorts of subjects.

This whole 'calling' of mine had started, consciously, for me as a boy when in a Bible class things came alive in an exciting way and I assumed that I had received both an encounter and a call. Because of the language and ethos of the Bible class I assumed that the encounter was with Jesus and the call was to serve God. As I understood it, God was for me in Jesus. I ought therefore to be for God, and this involved sharing with other people that God was for them. For the understanding, message and conviction was that God in Jesus was for all. (As we go on, we shall notice a tension between what might turn out to be an intensive sectarian approach to God being for one and calling one, and the extensive gospel: the good news that is really from the God of all for all.) Anyway, I believed that I had experienced an encounter and a call, and I simply got on with it in a great variety of ways, many of them exceedingly exciting, rewarding and promising.

However, in my sixtieth year I was invited to be the Bishop of Durham. Quite immense publicity followed from this. (I should mention, in passing, that this publicity originally arose around a television programme in which I was explaining as clearly and decisively as possible how nowadays I maintained the orthodox belief that the man Jesus was indeed and in very truth God with us and God for us.) As a result of this and much that followed from it I was subjected, and continue to be subjected, to very many invitations. All this calls me in question. How should I respond? What should I do? What is the whole 'Durham affair' really all about?

Ought I to respond to defend myself? That just does not seem good enough. First, it isn't really possible to defend oneself once various misrepresentations and misunderstandings have got around. To reach the heart of a matter requires much more sympathetic and open exploration and conversation than is possible at the height and in the heat of a controversy. Secondly, whatever this whole business was and is all about is something to do with Jesus. Now it is quite clear that Jesus was not in the business of defending himself. Therefore to pursue things for the sake of defending oneself when these things are somehow or other to do with an attempt to follow Jesus or be on the same wavelength as Jesus or to be picking up the God of Jesus is not appropriate. Thirdly and finally, to defend oneself is not all that important anyway when you have come to see – as you do see as you get older – that you are bound to die. In the face of death, much becomes relativized, and it comes to seem a good thing to choose what is really important. This is reinforced for me by the fact that I now have six grandchildren, all of whom seem to me to be singularly attractive and promising. Defending myself from various misunderstandings or the attacks of disturbed religious people does not seem to be very relevant to questions about their future. So I am pretty clear that whatever my response is, it is not a matter of defending myself.

So secondly, is it just that I have an opportunity to sell my wares? What a chance I have been provided with! Here am I, trying to be a teacher and some sort of missionary, and suddenly I seem to get the public ear. But again, on reflection this does not seem to be quite good enough – at least not without very careful reflection about what the wares are. Certainly they are not in any sense 'mine'. Unless the whole series of events has a chance of being something about God, the whole point of it is contradicted and confused. Who wants to sell things about faith and life and love to people? They are things which really need to be shared and explored, and they certainly do not belong to anyone in particular, so they are not really 'sellable'.

But if I were trying hard to convince people, could it be because I need, perhaps desperately, to convince myself? If that were the case, the selling would be far more about me than about the wares or the encounter with God. In that case there would be some sort of confidence trick mixed up with some sort of self-deceit. And that brings me to a third point.

No one, neither other people nor myself, ought to be deceived. Somehow or other realism is what matters. We must do our utmost to face things as they really are. Furthermore, this is what is owed to other people as persons and to oneself as a person, and this is what is to be pursued and shared. (I shall not claim to live up to or live out properly the various insights I try to share with you; the point is to share the possibilities and the challenges, not to make any claims about how one succeeds in responding to them.)

So why do I respond as I do – accepting invitations to speak and speaking in public – and, after reflection, decide that I ought to, must, want to go on doing so? The best answer I can give at the moment is this: because of *the problem of good, the glimpse of glory and the possibilities of God*. I find myself caught up in what I can best, but inadequately, describe as a love affair with a 'mysterious artist'. 'Love affair' is not an adequate phrase because it is not simply – or even mainly – a matter of my 'being in love'. There is a very strong undertow of attracting, desiring and longing; but it is much more a matter of having a sense of being loved and, even more, of being given a chance of becoming involved in a love affair which is really about affairs of love which are meant to embrace, involve and fulfil everything. That is to say, one has a share in the love so that one may share in the loving – in the sense of extending it and enabling it to be more and more real. And the reason for trying to talk about 'a love affair with a mysterious *artist*' is that the whole business is to do with not merely sharing but actually building up that which is shared – and that which is to be shared. The work of the artist is nothing like finished. There is something to be created and someone, somehow, to be creative with.

This is the background of my reference to *the problem of good*. There is so much of worth, of excitement, of value around in people and in things – whatever the threats and the negatives which we shall have to consider before we are finished – that one cannot just ignore this problem of good, or let things be or go on as if one had not noticed.

To spot the problem of good is to get an occasional *glimpse of glory* – that is to say, to see or feel something so attractive and worthwhile, so awe-inspiring, wonderful and celebratory that one knows that it must be pursued, cherished, built up and followed. Such glory may come through people – people with human faces are a special focus and provocation of glory – but it may also come through music, through colours, through the world, in the remoteness of the country or in the coloured feathers of a town bird; through intellectual excitement and discovery; through a stillness in oneself; or in a host of other ways. It is not a question of a utilitarian meeting of a need, but of an offer and a wonder which just is, and is to be enjoyed and followed.

Such moments, as I understand things, are hints of *the possibilities of God*. Therefore I am concerned, in one way despite myself and in another with all the commitment of my emotions, my will, my intellect and my spirit that I can muster, to share in the sharing of God.

But what on earth does all this mean, and how can it be entertained or pursued as a realistic possibility?

One way of trying to take matters further would be to set things out in terms of a pattern and a story which those who find themselves involved in a Christian church, or a group of Christians and sympathizers, come to know through the Bible. This is the proper and necessary way for me to proceed, because this is how I got on to the possibilities of God or, perhaps better, this is how the possibilities of God got hold of me.

I have joined others in discovering that what Christians called the Old Testament is a normative and formative record of what it is to be touched by God. Here is the record of a people, a community which is called and chosen by God. In this context I should refer back to my own personal sense of encounter and call to which I referred earlier. This repeated sense of encounter and experience builds up in those who have it the conviction that our God is the Lord. That is to say that he is a power of holiness, righteousness and steadfast love which is at work in and through all things, and we are part of these universal purposes. I want to stress the severity of this notion of love. It goes with holiness and righteousness (justice) and it must therefore have what might be described as a wrathful side. As love is determined to go for the best for all it must also be against that which works against the best for all. Hence the addition of the adjective 'steadfast'. We are not concerned here with something romantic in a weak sense – forgetful, unrealistic or indulgent – but with something very much tougher.

The whole experience of call, encounter and continuing relationship reinforces this sense of the Lord and of his purposes that we find in the Old Testament. The problem has to be faced that while he is the Lord, he has not yet established his lordship. Everything is not yet in accordance with his purposes and nature as holiness, righteousness and steadfast love. Nonetheless, as he is Lord and as he has called us to know him as such, we know that he will establish his Lordship. He really is the Lord.

A historical development in facing up to both this conviction about God and these problems about life in the world was the development of a variety of expectations about a 'messiah'. A messiah is someone anointed and appointed by God who will bring it about that his Lordship is established and that things are set up in accordance with his nature and purpose of holiness,

7

righteousness and steadfast love. (One way of talking about this is to say that his 'kingdom' will come.) Christianity came into existence because of the conviction of the first disciples of Jesus that Jesus was this messiah. This was brought about by the experience the disciples had with Jesus and their overwhelming sense after the crucifixion of Jesus that God has raised him up. In other words, he was alive and available to them in a way which showed that God had vindicated all that he was and all that he was committed to, and that this vindication by God was a defeat of the powers of death and of sin.

Here one has to face up to the really unexpected and disturbing nature of this discovery and conviction. For it turned out that the man who had cared for others and suffered for others, who had been crucified, dead and buried, was to be received as the way in which God established his lordship. This means that the lordship, the control, the power, the kingdom of God is like this. This is how God does what is expected of him in establishing his kingdom. Thus God has proved to be God in a totally unexpected way.

So for Christian believers like me, the possibilities of God have a revealed and promised pattern to match up to our personal intuitions and experiences, and one has to wrestle with bringing the two together. Since these possibilities and insights have become so buried in language which people nowadays find extremely difficult to follow, let alone to accept, I have struggled to produce simple ways of putting into words what I believe they are all about. Two of them can be set out like this:

God is. He is as he is in Jesus. So there is hope.
God is. He is for us. So it is worth it.

The point is that the discovery of God in and as Jesus is to make it clear that the hope of all and the worth of all are the worth and the hope of God. This is what is invested in the whole process of creation, and this is what we are called to discover and respond to.

It might be worth noting at this stage that Christian faith is not about Jesus; it is in fact about God. This follows because, as we can see from the Fourth Gospel and elsewhere, Jesus himself was not concerned with himself but with God. Now although this is a very particular discovery, it in fact has universal implications. What we are talking about and what we are seeking to respond to is the real and true God of the whole universe who has acted in Jesus to reveal himself for all, to get in touch with all and to reinforce his purposes of sharing and building up hope and worth for all.

All this is symbolized and summed up in a way of talking about God which is distinctive of Christian believing: the Trinity. God the Father is understood as greater than great, transcendent, mysterious and beyond all things, before all things, the end of all things. He is seen as equally present and real in his Son Jesus who is more loving than love, down to earth, alongside us, for us and committed to all that we are involved in, for the purposes of God and of love. God the Holy Spirit is God closer than close, dwelling within us, working between us and very much part of the fabric of things. Therefore we have God the Father, God the Son and God the Holy Spirit, all one and the same God, but it is necessary to speak about his mystery and his involvement in this differing number of ways. There are clearly problems here about language, not least about how we shall eventually reformulate the rather over-masculine formulation of this. (God is, of course, both he and she and beyond all that.)

So here we have a particular tradition and community of communities who claim to have experienced a particular set of calls and encounters which tell them things of vital importance about God, all as part of a pattern of revelation and activity by the God at the heart of things who is seeking to get in touch. One way of describing this state of affairs is to refer, as I have done, to the 'mysterious artist' with whom we can collaborate and share.

But will this stand up to where we now are both with regard to the world and with regard to religion?

With regard to the world I mean: how do we relate all this to the understandings of science, which are so often thought to clash with religious approaches to the world and certainly have been in conflict with the way religious people have claimed that you must approach the world? (Though there are many signs now that we have to look at things quite differently.) How does this very particular and personal way of seeing the mysterious and transcendent God in his relation to the world fit in with the size and scale of the universe as we now see it? And how does such an approach and a faith respond to and stand up to all the evil and randomness in the world?

With regard to religions I mean: how do we cope with the varieties of religions that are around in the world, especially when we examine things more closely and see that they do not easily converge and would seem to conflict over certain things. Further, various religions of the world have actually got into conflicts in practice, many of which do not seem to be at all godly. Then there is the worry of all the superstitions and unrealities that seem to appear in the practice of the various religions, not least Christianity. And finally there are the actual contradictions and evils which religions have brought into the world and seem to continue bringing into the world. It cannot be said at all unambiguously that religions and faiths are good things.

Now I am quite clear that there is nothing like a complete or satisfactorily decisive answer to questions and problems like these – both about the world as a whole and about religions in general. Faith is faith, and is neither protected by decisive argument nor established on guaranteed or guaranteeing grounds. You or we have to make up our minds. You or we have to decide where we commit our spirits and our hopes. You or we have to respond, to explore and to seek where we think we have been touched, provoked or found – often in the face of many counter-indications and difficulties.

I shall be going on to consider the matter of faith in God in more detail in the next chapter, and then I shall try to consider a little further some actual practices of responding to, exploring into and seeking out God in a chapter which takes some account of what I would call the pathologies of religion. For the moment, I have three further observations to make.

First, it seems nonsense to decide in advance or on *a priori* principles that glimpses of goodness and glory, or experiences of encounter and call, are less real or less significant clues to reality

10

than anything else or everything else that happens to us. Why set science and technology and rationalistic common sense over against love and art and wonder and readiness for suffering, risk and disciplined dreaming? All are human experiences and all are human encounters with whatever there is in the world, beyond the world, and at the heart of the world. Must a technical scientist cut more ice than a poet, or an organized problem-solver cut more ice than a saint? Can we not and might we not risk following glory, cherishing good and seeking God?

Secondly, there is a very strong and continuing tradition of people across all ages and cultures who are people responding to mystery and faith. They have to do so as individuals, for there has to be, for each one of us, our own commitment, response and faith. But that is not an individual thing. There are communities, there are writings (scriptures), there are practices of worship and there are disciplines of spirituality. Help and advice are available and communities are available for glimpsing glory, cherishing good and seeking God. There is much contradiction and confusion in these communities, but perhaps this is part of the human condition and one of the conditions of our responding and seeking for ourselves and in freedom. Creative artistry which is mysteriously seeking an achievement and a fulfilment through everything – and a fulfilment which is as yet beyond everything – may be a very risky business, not least perhaps because it is to do with genuinely open love and genuinely open freedom.

This brings me, finally, to Jesus. If it should be the case that in some real sense Jesus does represent and embody – within the particularities of the sort of history and humanity that we have to live through – the purpose and power and possibility of the mystery who is at the heart of things, then it would be clear that a good God is almost incredibly committed to risk, almost incredibly open and suffering love, almost incredibly involved in identifying with and being part of what goes on, what goes wrong, and what never ceases to have promise, although it always lives with threat. The Christian churches, of course and evidently, do not live up to this and frequently contradict this – but it may be that they just about serve to keep the possibility and the provocation alive.

11

It may be, therefore, that there are ways of discipleship and exploration open for those who would choose to be provoked by the problem of good, to pursue glimpses of glory and risk finding, and being found by, the possibilities of God. It may still be the case that a principal cluster of these ways of discipleship is to be found around and in association with the worship of God: Father, Son and Holy Spirit. But to find out we have to risk joining in, put up with the messes and muddles that Christians make, and see where we get to or where, as I believe, God will take us.

2

One World – Any Future?

In the previous chapter I described how I came to believe myself to be touched by God through experiences of encounter and call within the Christian tradition which resulted in my being concerned with the problem of good, glimpses of glory and possibilities of God. There are so many good, wonderful and exciting things around in the world, especially clustered around men and women, that I feel obliged to pursue glimpses of glory and the possibilities of God. These possibilities of God have been offered to me through the Christian tradition of God: Father, Son and Holy Spirit. They are possibilities of a God who is greater than great and wholly mysterious, a God who is more loving than love expressed in Jesus and very down-to-earth, and a God who is closer than close, the Spirit within us and between and very much involved with us.

But the question is: how does all that relate to or tie in with our actual condition in the real world? I began by starting from experience of God; now I want to start from our experiences of the world.

These include those famous pictures from space that show that it is indeed one world, and a limited world. We are threatened by our over-use of resources and by the ways in which we make life unendurable, or possibly unsustainable, for one another.

Moreover we get pictures all the time from our television which show that it is one world riven by division and threatened by starvation. There are all those continuing pictures of famine: and particularly striking of late, there are all those pictures of barbed wire. The first time I noticed it was when I saw television pictures of the Archbishop of Canterbury and Archbishop Tutu visiting Soweto. The barbed wire separated the township for the 'civilized' area outside it and around it. This was at the time when there were reports of the ways in which the United States was very bothered about its border with Mexico. It was becoming more and more impossible to prevent the pressures of the poor from Mexico spilling over into the affluent promised land of the United States. Were they going to be able to keep them out? Then we have the pictures of conflict and division and barriers in Northern Ireland. Along with that we have the barriers and the chaos in the Lebanon. We also know that our own country is very divided. 'North/South divide' may not be the way to describe it, but with all the insistence that we get from some quarters about choice and the freedom of the individual we are also faced with the very sharp question: choice for whom? Who are able to own their own houses? Who are able to choose education for their children? Who, indeed, are able to get jobs? We are confronted with the facts of poverty versus the facts of production and economic activity.

Most strikingly, on the one hand there is the City of London with all its affluence and flourishing and practically next door there are the problems of the inner city.

Finally (and this may be finally indeed!) all this is occurring when we are confronted with the nuclear arms race. We have the real threat of the possibility of the use of these abominably destructive weapons. We have the imbecility of their cost. Sometimes one is inclined to wonder whether, if there is a God of justice and of love, he may not decide that we deserve to be blown up when we are so wastefully using our resources in the face of so many demands of poverty and need. Then there is also the proliferation of risk as weapons get more complicated, systems get more sensitive and more people are on the verge of being able to set off nuclear explosions. Surely, therefore, it all looks very hopeless. At least it looks hopeless for anything else other than a quick buck for those who can make it while they can make it. 'Let us eat,

14

drink and be merry for tomorrow we die.' Consume while you can, if you can and that is that.

Now surely, in the name of God, in the name of all people who have human faces, in the name of our selves, this is not good enough. If there is any positive problem of good, if there are any glimpses of glory, any possibilities of God, then they must be pursued. But what difference could we expect God, and our response to God, to make? Would we expect sufficient miraculous obedience to the urgency of nuclear disarmament to bring about a miraculous universal dismantling of nuclear weapons? Surely not. Through whatever means, we have to pursue the building up of trust, the negotiation of limits and the eventual rolling back of the threatening threshold we are at. Here we have to face and answer for ourselves the basic and disturbing question about the nature of the world we live in and the nature of God, if any, that we see a possibility of, believe in and try to worship. I believe in God. I further believe that the God I believe in is the God pointed to by the basic patterns and promises of the Bible, the God who embodied himself as one of us in Jesus. I do not find any sufficient evidence in the Bible or in subsequent history which encourages me to believe that God is a large-scale worker of moral miracles whereby the stuff and struggles of our lives are rapidly and easily transformed into simple goodness and enjoyable peace. From the time of the first great prophets of Israel onwards at least, it has been plain that religious and moral demands on their own have never been sufficient to turn a society or group of any size from developing destructive ways to pursuing constructive ones. Repentance is an insight and an offering of the few which they have to contribute to the whole struggle. Here is a call arising from an encounter, an engagement with and a glimpse of the glory of God. The redirection to replanning of the many in a society, or of the whole of society, comes about through a bewildering and inextricable mixture of some creative moral and religious insights with the pressures of prudential self-interest, fear and force. We have no grounds, therefore, for expecting (still less relying on) miracles of conversion, and transformation brought about by some single great gesture or one item of policy. We must hope and

15

work for miracles of patience, survival and the creation of yet one more chance.

We are all in this one world and all under the aegis or the threat of what the USA and the USSR do, and we cannot opt out by a simple declaration of intent. What we have to do is to protest against the way in which both sides identify their systems and their approaches to the world as absolute and to be maintained without compromise. There is nothing so blasphemous or faithless as saying 'better red than dead'. Under God and, I would argue, under any reasonably humane view of the world and our prospects in it, our conflicts, great as they are, would be relativized. Today it is literally 'vital' (a matter of life and death) to be able to appreciate the point of view of those whom we have real reasons both to distrust and to resist. Our opponents, like us, are clearly seriously threatened. Like us they are human beings trapped in a deeply threatening world. It is one world, and we all contributed to its threatening nature by various versions of ideology, sin and indifference. We have to face up to the simple threat of death on us all with its terrible clarity, and in the light of this to negotiate our way through the complexities of life. And in this challenging demand we may well find and be found by God – who is as he is in Jesus – committed to encountering real evil and committed also to the worth of all and hope for all.

Some of the practical considerations which arise from the arguments outlined above include the following. First, there is no sufficient case for Britain's retaining 'an independent deterrent'. It obscures our actual and total dependence on the wider US and NATO alliances. The case for having our own deterrent looks like a false and dangerous fantasy produced by that sort of independence and aggressive nationalism which is precisely one of the main contributors to the threat of death which faces us all. Arguments about and efforts for maintaining our deterrent distract attention from our main and vital concern for policies of survival and then reconciliation. And the waste of resources in the face of our local as well as global poverty is monstrous. Secondly, we have nevertheless to retain our membership of NATO, and the process of giving up our own deterrent must be part of negotiations

16

within that alliance. There can be no substitute for continuing, uncertain and compromising negotiations. There is no magical, miraculous stroke which will, overnight, multiply the chances of peace. Peace is a possibility derived from costly, hopeful and faithful persistence deriving from a realistic awareness both of the threats and the possibilities.

Thirdly, everyone must be constantly reminded that the two over-riding pressures upon us are the threat of death and the necessity of having to live together. The over-riding aim of arms negotiations, therefore, is the prevention of war, not the prevention of victory by the other side or the achievement of victory by our own. The immediate prize to be aimed at is survival and the opportunity to live together in the hope of better things. This means, for example, that negotiations about arms limitations must be based on *quid pro quos* about arms restrictions and inspections. Extraneous demands concerning such matters as human rights or withdrawal of influence from this country or that are not part of negotiating improvements in our chances of survival. They are separate matters to pursue as we survive.

Fourthly, on a broader front, more and more attention should be concentrated on the issues of economy and poverty. The relativizing of our ideologies under the threat of death ought to help us to see that we do not have a crisis of capitalism with a saving Communism waiting in the wings. We have a total industrial and economic crisis; the Communist countries are sharing in the crisis of production, and all of us are without the means or the will to organize ourselves to share resources effectively in a way which will also multiply resources and at the same time protect the earth. A principal prudential reason, therefore, for negotiating arms reduction and mutual systems of control is the crippling burden of cost. Neither the US nor Russia can afford much longer the consumption of such huge resources, nor can the rest of us. This is one more way in which pressures of self-interest and fear could come together with such moral insights and hope as we can muster to move us in a creative and morally desirable direction. God has more resources than *our* faith and *our* morals. Every negotiation, pressure group or campaign for wider welfare,

17

justice or freedom is a worthwhile contribution to the human struggle for sufficient peace to enable survival, growth and search. As the Bomb makes it clear that we must live together, it may also free us to find better and more just ways of living together. Thus our last chance may still be our best chance.

Here, I believe, we may detect the presence of God in judgment for the sake of mercy and hope. The pressures upon us are not necessarily hopeless. They may lead to hope; they may be received, with the help of God, as practical, pressing and prudential pressured towards one world – one surviving and creative world. Of course some 'religious' people may think and give the impression that the difference that God makes is the difference between my disappearing when the nuclear explosion turns me into radioactive dust or my having some possibility of a future or continuing existence as myself, in relation to other selves and God. Christian faith suggests that this is one of the differences that God makes, or may make, but surely that is not what God is or what God is 'for', so to speak. The point, value, meaning, of God's existence cannot lie in his being my insurance policy or even in his being the survival of the one hundred and forty-four thousand who shall be saved. To believe such a thing is clearly a mere projection of my fear of death or my self-centred tribalism on to the mystery, the terror, the apparent nonsense and the evident glory of the universe. No doubt in the biblical and Christian tradition God is the God who saves. This we who are convinced Christians know in and through Jesus Christ by the power of the Spirit. But he saves because he is God. He is not God in order to save. Such a God would simply be an idol, a tribal deity, a human fantasy and protection. God, the Lord, the One Who May Not Be Named, the Creator, Redeemer, fulfilment of all that is or can be or will be, must be far more. As the holy, righteous and unutterably glorious One, God must be the worth and splendour and glory and beauty of all things, in all things and beyond all things. As he has shown himself in his steadfast love of Israel and in his passionate incarnation in Jesus Christ, believers know that he is the ultimate worth and worship who makes always for more worth and for shared worth. We who are his worshippers, called

18

by his grace, touched by his love and given glimpses of his glory know that he is the source and resource and inexhaustible depth of holiness, righteousness and steadfast love. Therefore he is concerned with, and full of, far more than my salvation or yours. The wonder is that he is also concerned with my salvation and yours — and of all. For that is the clear thrust of the New Testament. Christ died for all and God is for all so that the gospel must be preached to all.

But how can this be so, seeing the sort of place the world is and the sort of place we have made it? Is glory to be overcome by nuclear winter? I think we must be clear that the 'quite possibly' of nuclear destruction sharply confronts the 'surely not' of faith. Faith can only stand under the cross and go on to claim that God is indeed the worth in all things that makes for more worth and for shared worth; that is to say that he is indeed Love, in creation, in practice and in eternity. But he is more. He is the love, the righteousness and the mystery who for the sake of shared worth risks all that is against worth and takes on the cost, the agony, the passion, the mysterious and terrible threat, of all the anti-worth, all chaos, all absurdity, death and ultimate nothingness. The cross is the sign and promise of our salvation but it is so because it is far, far more. It is God's declaration of his total commitment to all that has happened and will happen because he has risked sharing his worth in holiness, love and true freedom.

Therefore faith understands and claims and hopes and lives by God as Creator, Redeemer and Sanctifier, of all things and to all eternity. As this is so, what difference does God make to the possibility of nuclear destruction? First, he provides the certainty that such destruction need not happen. Quite possibly there is no future, but this need not be so. Reagans and Gorbachovs and Thatchers do not have the last word about anything, never have had and need never have. This is the message of biblical books like Daniel or the Apocalypse, quite as much as the simple message of a simple faith in God in his mystery and love. Every effort at a wider, more generous and more hopeful view of the world, like every urgent action and struggle for peace, has its chance. No chain of events need reach its apprarently inevitable end until midnight has struck. Under God we always live at five minutes to midnight. Urgency is demanded, but fatalism and hopelessness is forbidden.

Secondly, God is the ultimate source of the resources by which, in a multitude of ways, distrust, selfish power, narrow self-interest and self-centred incompetence can be challenged and worked against while neighbourliness is developed, justice is sought, insults are suffered and patient endurance is developed. It is amazing how men and women can and will rally for helping one another, for facing disaster, for developing new ways of coping with problems and possibilities. The fire of creative love, the insights of our needs for one another, and the visions of a better world and more co-operative societies are never quenched. This is so because God is not ready to be defeated – and we who are in his image sometimes and sufficiently know this.

This seems to be the message of the possibility of God, and it is a message of hope about one world. All the pressures – nuclear pressure, ecological pressure, poverty pressure, the limitations of the market economy and the increasing stupidities of global credit – all these things can be lived with and turned back towards living together, building community, striving for efforts once again to move towards a sustainable world, a more just world, a more convivial and sharing world. If this is a dream, there is some evidence that God shares this dream with us. The threats are very much there, but so are the promises, and I would suggest to you that the God who commits himself to us in and through Jesus Christ is calling us to join him in facing the threats and in so doing to pursue the promises.

3

Towards a Renewal of Mysticism and Politics

We began by considering the possibility of being touched by, and being in touch with, a good God. Then we saw how the threats to our frail and one world, and the possibilities of our building and sustaining this one world, can themselves be understood as pressures of this good God upon us. I tried to argue that it is quite possible that our last chance is our best chance.

What I have been trying to concentrate on and look at from different aspects is what I would call the *issue of worth and hope*. Now in their traditional language Christians have called this the issue of salvation, but the traditional language has, mostly, gone dead on us. We – we Christians – certainly need the help of other God-fearers and God-searchers in our world to renew our language and to bring alive again the great and the universal power of the gospel as we understand it. I think that the traditional Christian language has tended to go dead because Christians right across the spectrum (all churches and all denominations, especially, I think, in Europe and the United States) have for years – perhaps for a century or two – allowed their practice of Christianity to become more and more cultic and more and more individualistic.

By cultic I mean that it has become more and more focussed on things like going to church, where you hear about, talk about and pray to a God who is described in special language which becomes increasingly peculiar to the cultic groups concerned. People have misunderstood the Authorized Version translation of I Peter: 'you are a peculiar people.' In a sense, 'by God we are!' And so what they have done has become peculiarer and peculiarer. Therefore it has looked more and more as if people were really concentrating on a rather peculiar and tribalist God.

So Christianity has begun to look like the cult of particular groups of people who in a way like things as they have become. This is underlined by the fact that Christianity is not just a cult but also a set of cults. This finally became focussed in my mind when I spent a number of weeks in Wyoming. I was staying about fifteen miles outside a small town, up a dirt road. When you drove into the small town you found that as you drove down the one street – and they still had the stores with the rails to which you tied your horses, and so on – first of all you came to a gas station and then you came to a brand of hamburger joint and then you came to a Christian church of one sort; then you came to another gas station, another hamburger joint and a Christian church of another sort. It was quite clear that gas stations, hamburger stations and spiritual gas stations were chosen according to taste, and possibly according to subscription. All this is just too cultic and separated and individualistic for words.

Christianity has also become more and more individualistic: there is a great deal of talk about *my* soul, *my* spirituality, *my* ethics and *my* future. One of the things which has shocked me in my own diocese is the degree to which people say: 'Oh, you can't have that sort of clergyman in there. It's not the right sort of churchmanship; it wouldn't be their flavour.' And that is thought to be a fairly absolute bar against an appointment. If I had the courage I would simply blow up and say, 'Good God! What has *that* to do with God?'

So Christianity has become cultic and individualistic, and people complain that their needs are not met. As if God might not want totally to revolutionize their needs! Now of course this sort of cultic particularity and individualistic turned-inwardness is quite clearly a travesty of what the God of the various Christian cults is really about. He is, and he is acknowledged to be in the various Christian cults, God the Father, God the Son and God the Holy Spirit (i.e. God who is greater than great; God who is more

22

loving than love; God who is closer than close and the God of all for all). So the cultic performance that goes on is a gross diminution of what the typical language of the Christian cults is really saying – or was originally saying in what we may call the biblical language.

In the biblical language and the biblical stories particular people are discovered by God or receive revelations of God at particular times and in particular circumstances, but what was being revealed was about the nature and the future of the whole universe and all people. As I said right at the beginning, there is a constant tension between this particular calling and particular receiving and particular responding and the fact that it is about the God of the whole earth. That is one of the reasons why he is constantly unexpected. But in practice, whatever may be the actual dynamics of the original language and the insights, this narrowly cultic and congregational activity is what being a Christian is mainly focussed on by the vast majority of Christians in this country, whether they call themselves Catholic or Anglican or Protestant or what you will. The principal sign and symptom of this is that going to church (if I may say so – and I speak with feeling because having become a bishop I now have to go to church far more than I ever would have done or think is necessarily healthy) is either a bore or a spiritual ego-trip. At least, it is a bore for anyone who has not become habituated to it so that it gives them a little comfortable, customary anaesthesia.

We must not be too solemn about it but, on the whole, going to church – coming together as Christians – is not something which more than a small number can possibly be expected to do; and I, for one, do not blame them. Going to church, taking part in church affairs generally, on the whole is not exposure to an exploration into a mysterious and attractive, awe-inspiring and ever-deepening reality. On the whole going to church and being attached to various church affairs forms a series of operations which protect us from the realities around us. The whole process tends to make people less human and less realistic. I once saw a poster up outside a place I was driving through which said 'Come to church'. I had a great sense that I ought to get out and put up another poster which said: 'This is the *last* thing you should do.' Which, I still think, is right. People have to know quite a lot about God before they can stand up to going to church.

So much church-going is just religious practices and not godly living and godly exploring. Something seems to have gone very wrong. I believe, as so often in the history of the church and of the various communities which go to make up the church, that just as God is bringing pressures upon us about one world, so he is bringing pressures to bear on us which could and should reawaken us to the immense God possibilities which are around in the world and in people and in the church. I would not be a bishop if I were not absolutely clear that even the church cannot keep a good God down. This is a fundamental axiom, as far as I am concerned. We ought to be reawakened to the powerful resources and insights which are available in and through the biblical records and in and through the various Christian traditions – if only we will not shut them up in the practices of religion.

In the first of these chapters that make up Part One I said that Christianity is basically not about Jesus. It is about God. For that is what Jesus was and is about. Similarly, the church and the churches are not about religion, though they get turned into religious cults; they are about God. They are about God in his concern for, and commitment to, the world. They are about the purposes, the possibilities of God which go far beyond the world and the churches. This is why I have given this third chapter the title 'Towards a Renewal of Mysticism and Politics'.

Let me try and explain. Traditional Christian language has largely gone dead on us. Internally it has gone dead on us: it is a sort of communal chanting which cheers some people up, anaesthetizes others, but does not actually allow us to relate it much to real life and does not look much further into life outside or do much about deepening spiritual life. It has gone dead on us externally. If you are having an argument, say, about politics, and someone says: 'but that is theological', it means it has become irrelevant, theoretical and mystifying. The church, if it is called in aid in the headlines of a paper or by a politician, is seen at best as being there to tell off the baddies. ('It is about time that the

Archbishop of Canterbury appeared on television and told off all these people who are bringing indiscipline into our inner cities. What we want is discipline!') Religion goes with reading, writing and arithmetic and keeping people under control. It is also pretty clear that there are many religions and none of them are other than minority occupations.

So, as the language has gone dead we really have to strip it down; to strip it down to phrases and patterns that will truly mean something to us. The First Letter of Peter says that you ought to be able to give a *logos*, which means an account of, or reason for, the faith that is in you. That does not mean reciting the mandalas which you have been taught but saying in words that mean something to you whatever it is that means something to you in relation to people whom you care about. Therefore you have to strip it down to language which really means something and which gets people going in an engaged and an engaging way.

In the first chapter I also suggested two mini-creeds which indicate in more comprehensible language than that of the historic Christian tradition what Christianity is all about:

God is. He is as he is in Jesus. So there is hope.
God is. He is for us. So it is worth it.

(Just in case it should be thought that these statements are not really Christian, doctrinal, biblical or whatever, let me explain that the first one is about the doctrine of the Trinity and eschatology, and the second one is about the doctrine of the atonement and sanctification.)

God is the transcendent, mysterious, ultimate possibility of things, the reality of realities, the beyond, the within and that which is to come. He is as he is in Jesus. The Son who has been one with us as man has died for us and has risen. So there is hope. There is a power at work, largely to be experienced in the Spirit, which simply cannot be got down by anything that anyone or the world will do. As Paul put it in chapter 8 of his Letter to the Romans: 'There is nothing in death or life, in the realm of spirits or superhuman powers, in the world as it is or the world as it shall be, in the forces of the universe, in heights or depths that can overcome the love of God in Jesus.' There is nothing such things can do, so there is hope. And that is eschatological, because it means that things are actually going towards some worthwhile end. Not only that, but we can be part of that end and contribute to that end and be caught up in that end.

God is; he is for us. That is the doctrine, if you like to call it so, of the atonement. The doctrine of the atonement is a collection of myths, stories and explanations which show the different ways in which people have discovered that God is prepared to take upon himself the shortcomings, the contradictions of human existence so that we can actually be one with him and part of him. Therefore life is worth it. None of the things which contradict the love of God or the loveliness of human faces, the glory of the world or the possibilities of all the things that are around need do so permanently. They are being confronted by the power of God himself, and therefore there is the possibility that this worthwhileness (which we know about and which in our best selves we want to promote and pursue) can actually be enjoyed in a community and communion of love. The world, and all the personal beings in it, are open to godly resources of holiness, righteousness and steadfast love. There is always hope, for God is. He is as he is in Jesus. He is at work. So there is hope. A source of hope is always available, for God is. He is for us, all of us, though we constantly keep going against him and against one another. So the worthwhileness of things is always around, always to be enjoyed and affirmed, always to be built on and always to be looked forward to.

As I began this chapter by saying, this way of talking picks up salvation language because it is talk about the possibility of being saved from what in the traditional language is called sin and what in untraditional language (which I get into trouble for using, but I think you have to do it) I call 'the buggeration factor'. By that I mean the way in which, just when things are going splendidly and someone has a really good idea, some idiot comes along, produces something idiotic and everything actually gets . . . up. Or again the very glory of things, the very fact that we depend on one another, is actually exploited. The very discoveries and developments which actually make it possible to feed the whole world – not quite tomorrow, but in about three months if things were organized properly – are actually used to build up butter mountains and make profits for people on what are called futures. I do not think that a phrase like 'the buggeration factor' is anything like strong enough for that sort of thing – the sort of thing sin is about. The message, the Christian message, and hope, and commitment in experience is that we can be saved from this. And that also means being saved from the fact that by behaving the way we do we alienate ourselves from one another and from ourselves. (I sometimes get a bit worried about talk of being saved to live with everyone for ever – I can't live with most people most of the time anyway, and as for living with myself, it can be intolerable! So obviously we have to be changed.)

We can be saved from the way things are with us, and far more importantly, there is not only the possibility of our being saved from everything that diminishes or prevents holiness, righteous ness or justice, and steadfast love; there is also the offer of being saved into all that promotes and enjoys holiness, righteousness, justice and steadfast love – and that is the most important thing.

We have been concerned, then, with salvation, with overcoming sin. So I would suggest that the whole of the biblical stories and the whole of the Christian tradition can be explored through phrases like: 'God is. He is as he is in Jesus. So there is hope.' One of the advantages of a phrase like that, I have already found, is that you can use it to discuss the possibilities of hope and worth in practice with people who are believers of other faiths or who are not believers. I have got into conversations of a practical and spiritual sort with people on the basis of 'God is'. They know that I believe that the way to God is Jesus, but I do not keep putting Jesus in the way. He never got in the way himself; he *was* the way. So we can keep to talking about God.

If people do not believe in anything like God, they are still very much concerned with hope, and a conversation is possible about how we hope and what we hope for. It may seem a risk to leave out God and Jesus, but if you have some basic understanding of the meaning of your faith, you are totally free to risk it. And that, of course, is exactly what Jesus did. The Gospel of John shows, I think very clearly, that the reason why Jesus was able to give himself away totally was that he was totally sure that he and the Father were one.

God is. He is for us. This is a reminder every time we get totally depressed. In a personal relationship, every time you are so depressed and oppressed that you think that the only thing you can do is totally to lose your temper, or totally to go into a sulk, or totally to turn your back on people, or totally not to try again, you are asked, 'But is it worth it?' The same feeling builds up, not only in personal relationships but in the business of running an institution. For instance, it may be necessary to bite one's tongue and hang on when a meeting is going in such a way that it would be absolutely splendid to break it up entirely, and it would probably be what the meeting deserved, but it has to be kept going, because otherwise how will the next meeting take place which might get somewhere? Usually it won't get anywhere, but nevertheless one has to keep trying.

It is worth it. And that feeling has to be built up further – and here we approach the area of politics. For instance, the minute it becomes clear to most people that there is no hope, or they think that there is no hope, of reconciliation between a United States approach and a Soviet approach, someone is going to get cross enough to press a button. But while there is a realization that it is worth it, and there is hope, there is a chance that this will not happen. These things are very practical and very spiritual. There is an offer of salvation from sin, and above all there is salvation into being part of this building up of the possibilities of God, people and world. But it will require, it does require, it has always required a multitude of organized and interlocking attempts at renewing mysticism and politics.

So we need a multitude of organized and interlocking attempts to renew mysticism and politics. By mysticism I mean rediscovering, and discovering, new ways of seeing and grasping and following up the conviction that we need spirituality. Mysticism is the sense that there is a chance of responding to goodness and glory and God, that there is a chance of exploring the depth, the breadth, the height, the possibilities of this. It is a matter of growth, exploration and depth. This sort of exploration and commitment is really related to the basic faith that at heart, and basically and hopefully, women and men are not either problem-solvers or consumers. They have a chance of being problem-solvers, and we are certainly very concerned with being consumers, but that is not basically what we are. Certainly people are not rubbish to be left on one side because they do not fit in with the forward movement of society, are a nuisance, or whatever. Nor are people absurd accidents. It is not true that, as Sartre said, man is a useless passion.

Men and women, women and men are in the image of God. That means that they are capable of resonating with, responding to, sharing in the mutual fulfilment of one another with that mysterious artist, lover and unnameable God who is holiness, righteousness and steadfast love. Therefore we must do all we can to be part of exploring and recognizing and developing what I am calling the mystical depths – and once we see the point we shall rejoice in doing so. (Though it will not be all rejoicing; if it is anything like following Jesus and many other of the saints and gurus that have been spread across the world, it will involve cost, suffering, uncertainty, lostness, wilderness.)

By 'exploring the mystical depths' I mean responding to the promptings and callings that we do get about there being much more worth and many more possibilities than we ever imagined. I mean responding to the visions we get that suggest how worthwhile it would be if we really could move in that direction, the callings we get to go on caring – though it is so easy to get involved in a set-up which is full of what seems incredible cynicism and greed. It is possible to go into, and seek to reach up to, the values and the visions. There are also what I would call the mystical moments and the mystical opportunities, the encounters that must be followed up, the glimpses that show what there really could be if people would stick at it.

One illustration of that is something I remember from changing planes once in North Carolina. Being fed up and far away from home I was feeling extremely depressed, and to make it even worse, in the corner of the waiting room there was a rather ugly woman with a snotty child. The child kept making tiresome noises and the mother kept on nattering at it in a way that was bound to make it worse. I started thinking: 'This is the end. The human race is so useless. Why do these people breed?' Then another plane came in and a man alighted, and as he came in through the room the face of the child and the mother simply lit up. This was dad. He was home, and everything was transformed. I suddenly realized that this is what things are really about. That is what I mean by a mystical moment. And when you see something like that you simply have to try to live by it.

That is what I am talking about, and I wanted to come back to earth like that to make it clear that being mystical in this way is not something refined and specialized, though of course there are people who find different ways of going deeper into this and who do become special people with special ways of teaching. But it isn't highly specialized. It is a human possibility to which we are open and which we can all follow up. Although I think that mysticism is not quite the right word, I could not think of a better one and I wanted to raise this question of being open to the possibility of contributing to the realities of life, to the openness of life, to the worthwhileness of life. In particular I am concerned with this because we are sometimes convinced (and when we are not convinced we ought to make an act of will to go on behaving as if we were convinced) that men and women, women and men, are simply 'more'. There is more to them and us and to everything than we can yet cope with or know. More than, for example, statistics – although this does not mean that we ignore statistics. If hundreds and thousands of people are on the dole, that is a statistical and structural problem which has to be tackled by structural and political action. It cannot simply be tackled by saying 'get on your bike and try harder'. It just cannot. So we have to have the statistics. I am not at all against statistics, sociology, analysis and the like. People who rush around in small circles saying 'You must love everybody', and exhaust themselves over the first three, are just an impracticable nuisance! They ought to conserve their energies and get things organized.

30

So people are more than just statistics and this fact has to be wrestled with in a quite costly and difficult way, working out policies for ways forward. People are more – and this is very important – than problems. I think I had a minor revelation once when I was travelling on a train in Java. I was doing so for the World Council of Churches under the auspices of the Indonesian churches and they kindly put me on a train to send me to the end of the island to talk to some people. As I was going across the island I suffered from claustrophobia. It is a tropical island with sunshine and bright light, and I suddenly got the terrible feeling that I would suffocate. There were so many people around and the whole countryside was either covered by rice fields or villages, or there were just barren mountaintops where nothing could be grown. I knew my statistics – a hundred and twenty million people, most of them so poor they were on the verge of starving – and I thought to myself: 'Nothing can be done about this.' And either the Lord, or Freud, or something I had remembered from reading it in a book said to me: 'Of course nothing can be done about this if you think of these hundred and twenty million people as a hundred and twenty million problems. But if you can help them think of themselves as a hundred and twenty million resources there is no knowing what you can do.' (Chairman Mao thought of that, as a matter of fact, but I do not see why Christians should not as well!)

People are more than problems. There is a tendency to analyse our North/South divide as though what has to be done is to tax the South-East a bit more in order to help the North, or the inner city, or whatever. No doubt redistribution of all sorts of fiscal means is necessary, but people are more than problems. And people are more than consumers. All the pressures nowadays turn people into consumers, persuade them to consume more by suggesting that unless more is sold (and by implication more is consumed) the economy will not take off. That is dreadful.

Beyond the economic dimension, people are also more than women, or more than men, though they are women and men: they are also more than black or white, but that does not mean that they are not black or not white. One has to take absolutely seriously what people are – but they are more than that.

31

Then again, people are more than professionals. They are certainly more than priests or bishops. One of the alarming things in the life of the church is that once people become priests or bishops they seem to think that they have a special role to behave in a priestly or bishop-like way and they cease to be human. So people are more, and this 'more' has to be worked with, worked for, looked into. That is what I mean by developing mysticism. It is going deeper into good, glory and God; going further into holiness, righteousness and steadfast love, and then more: more explorations of faith, more disciplines of spirituality, more practices of attention and waiting and risking.

Now my last point. I believe and hope that if we could develop on a wide front and in a wide variety of ways this sort of renewal of mysticism, it would also be part of a renewal of politics. In a basic sense, politics has to be recaptured. It is not the battles of particular parties, programmes and ideologies for power, though it is all that, because that is what happens in politics. Politics is basically about how we organize ourselves to deal with power and handle resources in order that human beings may survive and flourish. That is what *oikonomia* is in Aristotle: handling households so that they may flourish. *Oikonomia* has now become economics, which is very difficult to handle, but we must keep reminding ourselves what it is really about; the survival and flourishing of people.

If we have been concerned, through our practical mysticism, with going deeper and deeper into hope and into worth, then our activity must surely flow over issues like: 'How do we all experience hope? How do we all become aware of, and contribute to, hope, to worth?' That means engaging locally, in whatever things we come up against, or whatever concerns we feel called to, with regard to matters of worth. What are the things which destroy our neighbours' sense of worth? What are the obstacles which prevent people from knowing that they have worth, from contributing to a worthwhile life? What are the things around which promote worth and can be shared, and are not zero-sum games, but build outwards so that they are more and more shareable? What are the things which already cherish, sustain and maintain worth? There is a whole set of questions here, for example, about the way we ought to organize resources for health care, resources for social services, and so on and the realization that these resources should be put into sustaining those areas of society where people sustain one another. I am not talking about the cynical games that are played, like getting people out of hospitals so that they are no longer on the NHS budget but on someone else's (that can easily happen nowadays with the current cuts). I am talking, rather, about asking what one can do about actually building up the families, the neighbours, who care.

Some of these responses will be neighbourly, local and communal; others will be organizational, pressurizing and political. But if we pursue our practical mysticism out into our practical politics we shall discover, it seems to me, ways of contributing to neighbourly care and political action which are centred on people as worth it; people as entitled to be set free to contribute their own worth to the world of all. We shall be sharply reminded that any set of political bosses of course have to have a medium-term view, but they have to reckon with the fact that people are worth it *now*, not when they can afford to recognize the fact. This is the sort of pressure that has to be kept up. I think this could lead to a restoration and a renewal of what I would call *democratic and participatory politics* as opposed to politics which is largely manipulative, sells programmes to people and then forces them down their throats. We have a long way to go, but such politics can be revivable and discoverable. We shall all, it seems to me, have to challenge the individualism and the amazing centralization that goes with current Conservative politics. We shall all have to challenge the ideology and the sectarianism that goes with much left-wing politics. But above all, we have to challenge the apathy in our society about our politics and our prospects.

I had an interesting conversation with a taxi driver recently. Having recognized me, he confessed that he was not really interested very much in any party or any church because he did not think that anyone could do anything much about anything. This is the great challenge. How do we recover together some sense that there is hope, that it is worth it, and we might be able to work together for once? Particularly when it looks as if so many people think they have ceased to matter and are increasingly without hope, and more and more people are treated more and more as if they are of no worth. Quite clearly, I would suggest, mere politics, sheer politics, will not cope with this. We need to develop the salt which can restore savour to the whole. That may very well be done by entering on the renewal of mysticism and politics. We may need to hear this call to start on this and to keep going because we are prepared to follow up the problem of good, we are prepared to respond to the glimpses of glory, and we are prepared to risk the possibilities of God. All this in relation to the worth of all women and all men and to our commitment to the possibilities of the hope of a future which is nearer and nearer to God's future of holiness, righteousness and steadfast love.

I think that this is a Christian aim to pursue, for if we did become involved in this sort of thing, and if we did try and work this out in relation to our daily practical, neighbourly and social life, we would be responding to the two great commandments: Love the Lord your God with all your heart and with all your soul and with all your strength and with all your mind, and love your neighbour as yourself.

PART TWO

Rediscovering the Truth

THE MYSTERY OF GOD THE HOLY TRINITY

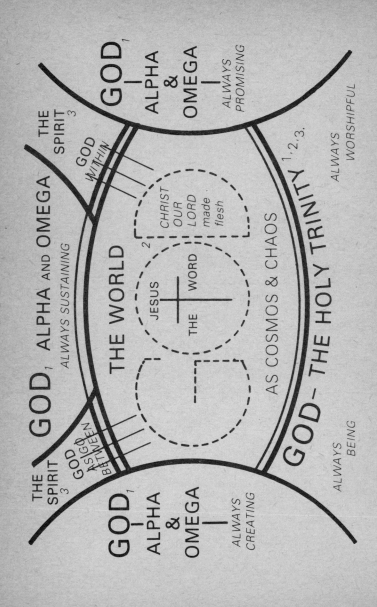

GOD₁ ALPHA & OMEGA
ALWAYS PROMISING

THE SPIRIT₃
GOD WITHIN

GOD₁ ALPHA AND OMEGA
ALWAYS SUSTAINING

THE WORLD

CHRIST OUR LORD made flesh

JESUS THE WORD

AS COSMOS & CHAOS

GOD – THE HOLY TRINITY¹,²,³
ALWAYS WORSHIPFUL

THE SPIRIT₃
GOD AS GOD BETWEEN

GOD₁ ALPHA & OMEGA
ALWAYS CREATING

ALWAYS BEING

4

Rediscovering the Truth about God

The diagram with which this chapter begins is meant to serve as a starting point for a number of reflections on our Christian faith. The hope is that one or more of these reflections will be of value, that they can be picked up and shared in as part of a common exploration. But before we look at it more closely, here are some preliminary remarks by way of introduction.

I feel very strongly, especially in these both very difficult and extremely exciting days, full of challenge and opportunity, that the church needs to recapture a sense that we are a people on a pilgrimage. We are a people on a pilgrimage because we have picked up that ultimate purpose and ultimate glory and ultimate promise which is invested in the world and in creation and in the whole of the universe. We are those who have been called to know something – specially called to know something – about the ultimate mystery that we call God and that necessarily means that we become engaged on a pilgrimage.

Unless we can move on and in and deepen our understanding of the wavelength we have picked up, of the sense we have begun to have, of the calling that we have received, of the excitement that we sometimes get, we shall not be anything like the part we are meant to be of the world at large. Nor shall we be able to play our part in the exploration of God and of what it means to be human.

So it is important that we should share in thinking about God, then about Jesus, then about people, and finally about the Holy Spirit and the church, as we shall be doing in these next four chapters.

When we ask what all this is about, I think that we can sum it up by saying that it is all about sharing in the sharing of God.

The church exists because a people emerged who became Israel and then the Jews. These people became increasingly convinced that there is a promise, a power, a possibility and even a personality behind things, invested in things and working through things, who is concerned to share that promise and power and personality so that in the end there will be something even more glorious than that with which we started. Among them there developed those who were convinced that Jesus was the Christ and therefore the clue to the further development and fulfilment of their convictions and hopes about God. Therefore we are concerned with sharing in the sharing of God. Now if that is what it is all about, then if we are engaged in looking again at the basics of pilgrimage in which we are engaged, we have to start with God.

Of course, the great hope and belief is that we shall *end* with God. Until we end with God we shall not really know; we shall be searching. The mystery which is around us and within us and beyond us and calling us and enticing us is a mystery which remains a mystery until we know as we are known. Then when we know, we shall still know that it is a mystery and know that there is more to know.

That, incidentally, is why eternal life will not be a bore. I have often thought to myself that I know that I should want eternal life because I am told that God promises it to me and of course it is impolite not to want what God promises. But I have often wondered whether going on and on and on wouldn't be an awful bore. Of course, if we went on and on as we are now we should soon discover, as Sartre put it, that hell is other people. We only have to look in a mirror to see that unless we are transformed, heaven will be hell, supposing we spend our lives there. That is why it must be transformation, growth and development. But I

38

have begun to get glimpses, especially through other people, that eternity could be infinitely worth it precisely because there will always be more to discover.

One way in which I picked this up was when I worked for the World Council of Churches and got increasingly frustrated over the language problem. How do you share communications with people who speak languages other than your own? There is a frustration over having to have everything conducted in most international gatherings in English, which is other people's second or third language. And that is particularly a frustration to me, with a Welsh ancestry, so that I rapidly get intoxicated by the exuberance of my own verbosity and go faster and faster, with the result that communication becomes very difficult. It occurred to me that one of the purposes of eternity is to be enabled by the grace of God to learn perfectly every possible language there is so that everyone can express themselves in such a way that they will be understood fully by other people and be able to share with other people. And there, as Humpty Dumpty might say, there is glory for you. There is an eternal possibility. So I am quite clear that heaven will not be a bore, because the mystery is infinite and there will always be more to discover.

However, we are not exactly concerned with heaven now but with God. We seek, it seems to me, to begin with God, and for Christians that means seeking to remind ourselves where the basics of our faith lie. And this means starting with God as God the Holy Trinity. For that seems to me to be *the* distinctive symbol of *the* distinctive Christian understanding of God. Of course there are all sorts of channels to God; but the really distinctive feature of the Christian understanding of God is the symbol of God as Holy Trinity: God the Father, God the Son and God the Holy Spirit.

Now to say that already lands us in trouble because we then have to go on to say that there are not three Gods but one God. The reason for that is quite clear: there is only one God to be. So while we may have to use threefold language, we are talking about the one God. This is the point at which mystery becomes mystification and muddle. Had I been lecturing in the introductory course which I gave when I was Professor of Theology at Leeds in the first year of Theology and Religious Studies, I would then have hastened to point out that you must clearly understand that God is a mystery so that language is difficult, and that when you say that there are three persons but one God you do not mean by 'person' what you mean by person and you do not mean by 'three' what you mean by three and you do not mean by 'one' what you mean by one! At which point everyone thinks that the matter is simple and clear!

Whereas there is bound to be confusion. If as you explore into the mystery of God you feel puzzled or confused, however, do not despair. There are certain simple things to fall back on.

The first is what we call 'the grace', which is actually II Corinthians 13.14: 'The grace of our Lord Jesus Christ and the love of God and the fellowship of the Holy Spirit be with you all.' We are in fact strongly in the habit of using trinitarian language about God, since we receive it as part of our worship, as part of our prayers, as part of our functioning: the grace of our lord Jesus Christ, the love of God, the fellowship of the Holy Spirit. And then there is 'the blessing', with which I am becoming increasingly familiar, since if I am not given anything else to do at a function, I am at least asked to pronounce the blessing: 'The blessing of God Almighty, the Father, the Son and the Holy Spirit, be amongst you and remain with you always.' These simplicities are always there to fall back on in our pilgrimage.

Now it is quite clear from all the saints and from much in the Bible that this pilgrimage into God is a pilgrimage from something we know towards something we hope to know through things we do not know. It is like love. It seems to me that one of the things you discover is how important love is as you begin to love, but once you really fall in love you begin to discover that you didn't know what love was. Then as you go on, if you go on, there are more and more demands, and more and more opportunities. One of the things about the growth in love is discovering that you have to love in different ways and new ways.

It is very much the same with discovering God, with the way

into God. The way to get closer to God lies through going into uncertainties which may make one feel that one is lost. Lostness on the way to God, finding that one has known God, is not sure that one knows him now but hopes that one will know him again, and therefore supposes that one does know him now – that sort of thing is very much a feature of spirituality and pilgrimage. Knowledge of God is really about prayer and faith and is very often a matter of having to wait, and then going on again into more knowledge and prayer and faith, then more waiting, and then going on again. Because if God is God, there is always more. But the tradition of the revelation of God through Jesus Christ in the Spirit is focussed in this understanding of God the Holy Trinity. That is why I have called the diagram, which we shall now look at more closely, 'The Mystery of God the Holy Trinity'.

You will observe that in the middle of the diagram, bounded by two thick lines, there is something which if you were thinking about it without noticing the title you might suppose was meant to represent an eye. However, that is purely coincidental and accidental. Please do not take the diagram too seriously and suppose that every part of it is significant.

In the middle of the diagram, bounded by the thick lines, is the world. That is because we start from the world in which we live and we are concerned with the world and with God. I have labelled this part 'The World', and put at the bottom 'As cosmos and chaos'. For the world as we experience it is a very mixed thing indeed. When we are experiencing the world rather more as chaos than as cosmos, and thinking that it is one damned thing after another, and wondering what it will come to, we may sometimes pray very hard; and if we are very fortunate and God is very gracious, something may then happen so that we find that the world is not one damned thing after another. But it doesn't get changed very much.

So we are confronted with, we find ourselves in and part of, the world which we experience in a mixed sort of way. One way of putting it, using Greek words which come out of the Bible, is to say that the world is cosmos and chaos. Sometimes you get an ordered pattern, which is what cosmos means, and the world seems to be going somewhere. And sometimes – more often than not – you experience it as chaos. Just as you are heading for a nice pattern, somebody comes along and turns it into chaos again. Just when you have a bright idea about finally getting the family organized, either you have to move or one of the children does one of those dreadful things which children do because they are actually growing and expanding – and no doubt being creative, except that their creativity doesn't quite fit in with your ideas. And the cosmos seems to be heading for chaos again.

Now one of the things which helps one to believe firmly in the God who is revealed in the Bible is to see how realistic and down-to-earth the Bible is. It, too, is aware that the world of which we are a part is a very mixed thing. We may note, for instance, that in the Bible God is always having trouble with the people who worship him. One phrase which crops up is 'The Lord has a controversy with his people' (e.g. Hosea 4.1). That is a great encouragement to me, because it seems quite clear to me that again and again the behaviour of the church is one of the greatest arguments against the existence of God. One finds that one cannot do without the church, but nearly two times out of three one finds that one cannot do with it either. I have formulated this into what I call my ecumenical slogan: 'Even the church cannot keep a good God down.' And I believe that to be a profoundly biblical observation.

The Lord has a controversy with his people. There is a battle going on, and the battle is as much about the abuse of religion as about anything else. That is certainly clear from the Old Testament, and even more so from the 'he came unto his own and his own received him not': Jesus was crucified by a combination of the civil authorities and the ecclesiastical authorities. This is something that we need to be reminded of very often, especially we bishops: without total grace there will be total hell.

In the midst of this mixed world there are signs and signals of the presence of God. That is what the Bible is about. People pick up signs of God, are able to interpret them as signals from God, and therefore a belief grows that is witnessed to in the Old Testament of a presence, a pattern, a promise which is involved in this world but goes far beyond this world, and give us hopes which, although they are encountered in the world, go outside it.

I have written round the left and right and top of the diagram the sort of things that people who have picked up these signs of God and signals from God come to believe that he is. And because of these signs of God and signals from God they come to believe, and commit their lives to the belief, that in the cosmos the ordering, the patterning and the promising has the priority over the chaos. If you look into even Genesis 1 you will see the Spirit of God brooding over the initial chaos and beginning to order it.

Therefore the belief grows that God is the beginning and end of things. So on the left-hand side of the diagram we have God the Alpha and Omega (the first and last letters of the Greek alphabet), always creating. The more we discover and believe from the signs of God and the signals of God, the more the conviction grows that he is a faithful God, a loving God, a concerned God, a God who is always conflicting with, and in battle with, the things that are against him and his ordering and his purposes. God as alpha and omega is not only thought of as always creating but, as I have put on the right-hand side of the page, as always promising.

As we receive these signs and signals in the world that there is this God who is always creating and always promising and often discover those signs and signals right in the middle of the chaos, where we receive new signs of cosmos and ordering and purposes, a great faith is gradually built up in a God who is always sustaining. I have put that at the top of the diagram. This is God at the beginning of things, God working through things and God at the end of things, because he is God who is upholding all things and working in all things.

This faith is an interaction between signs of God and signals from God on the one hand, and faith and response on the other.

It is an amazing faith in God, who will be faithful though he slay. You may sit by the waters of Babylon and weep; you may be so cross at the way in which you seem to have been abandoned by God that you long for a time when people will come and dash the children of your enemies against the stones (as Psalm 137 puts it), because that is what happened to your children. Yet despite these terrible things the faith remains that there is a God who is always creating, always promising and always sustaining.

This was the faith which became focussed in Jesus, the Word of God – that is why I have the cross in the middle of the diagram. We shall go on to Jesus in the next chapter; here I would just remind ourselves that this whole belief and under-standing of God as always creating, always sustaining and always promising was underwritten by the understanding and preaching of Jesus, and by what happened to him when that was crowned by the resurrection.

For the moment we continue our reflections on God. What Jesus was and what happened to him led on to the understanding that God was to be known not only through this experience that he was beyond things, sustaining things and promising things, but could also be known by that personal revelation of him and embodiment of him which is Jesus Christ, our Lord; be known also by that which followed on the life and resurrection of Jesus Christ: the discovery that he was indeed the Christ and was indeed risen. That was the gift of the Spirit.

That is what underlies the conviction that God is at all times to be understood as first the God who is beyond all things, the God who is always creating, always sustaining and always promising – and as such is always more. He is not confined to the particular things that are going on now, to the particular ways we experience him now, to the particular knowledge we have of him now. For he is the mystery behind things, the mystery working in things and the mystery towards which all things are working.

Thus God is other and everywhere, and the God who cares, and the God who comes. He gives signals, and Christianity came into being with the belief that he not only sends a variety of signals but finally sends the ultimate signal, that is himself, his word embodied in Jesus Christ.

The traditional and regular way of speaking about the God who is other and everywhere and who cares and who comes is 'God the Father'. But what took Christians a good deal of time to work out fully – and I suppose that we haven't worked it out fully even now; we certainly don't live up to it – was the discovery that this final word of his, in Jesus, is actually God giving himself under the conditions of history in the conditions of humanity. That means that the infinite, the transcendent, the mysterious and the glorious God, who is always creating, always sustaining and always promising, is also able to be, and chose to be, the man Jesus. Jesus is God with us and God for us. Therefore, our understanding of God in the mystery which is before the world and beyond the world and is always sustaining the world has to have built into it the understanding that God is so committed to his purposes of creation, so determined to bring about his promises, so utterly involved in sustaining, that he is also to be understood as God the Son.

The Son is embodied in Jesus Christ, and the Son became man, but the Son is as much God in every sense as God is God. He warns us, promises us, that it is not a mere metaphysical theory or a mere religious dream to say that God is love. God is love in being and in practice; in commitment, in capacity to be totally involved in flesh and blood. So we have not only God as other and everywhere, who cares and comes, the Father, but God who is in and as Jesus, the Son. The power and the dynamic of that was realized in practice and then reflected on in thought by the discovery that God was quite as much God when he was, as you might say, being or acting as the Spirit. But it is not a mere metaphor to say, as Paul does, 'know you not that your bodies are the temple of the Holy Spirit'. It has to be understood that the mystery is great; God is so much love and so much committed and so much concerned and so much saving that he dwells in us. Look sometime at the remarkable argument in Romans 8, where Paul is given the vision that we can call God our Father because we have been called in the Son to be part of the redeemed of God the

Father, and that means that God the Spirit is in us. There is a splendid verse in the middle of Romans 8 which says that 'the Spirit prays for people in God's own way'; we don't know, says Paul, how to pray. I think that when we get nearer to the heart of praying in the midst of cosmos and chaos and longing for love and so on, we are often embattled and inarticulate – what on earth should we pray for? But there is God within us, who, as Paul says, will take up our inarticulate groans and make them part of the whole longing and sustaining and work of God. The Spirit is praying within us – praying for God's own people in God's own way – because he knows the mind of God. For in a very real sense he *is* the mind of God.

There is God as other and everywhere, there is God in Jesus and there is God in and as the Spirit. This is what is offered to us in our Christian faith and by our Christian faith. If you ask, 'How do we know this?', the answer is, 'By becoming members of the community of faith who live by this faith and therefore seek to live out this faith and find ourselves living into this faith.' We have the witnesses and the stories of the Bible and the experience of the church. This building up of an understanding that there is another who is far more great and infinite and more mysterious than anything that is in the world and yet who is invested in the world. There is this one who comes and there is this one who cares; and it is possible to experience this otherness and this coming and this caring not only through and in the stories and the celebration of this Jesus Christ but also through and in the life of the Spirit. This is renewed again and again and gives us a pattern for our whole discipleship, our whole approach to the world. It invites us to be part of God at work through us and God at work between us. This is why people and the church play an essential part. This is why the church is essential even if we cannot do with it – because it is only as people are called to the whole community of people, as they pick up the God wavelength, as they find the God wavelength focussed in Jesus, as they live out of that in the Spirit – that there is a continuing witness. But we are not dependent on ourselves for the continuing witness, for it is the God who creates, who is the God who is incarnate in Jesus, who is God the Holy Spirit, who is there to make sure that the work goes on. So at every point, whether it be for our creation or for our sustaining, for our promising or for our knowing or for our serving, we are dependent on God now. God with us now. God working through us now. That is God the Holy Trinity, and we are reminded of that God again and again, whether we are being directed to the infinite mystery of the world and beyond the world and of love, or whether we are being focussed on the flesh and blood of Jesus Christ and on the particularity of the commitment of love to actual events and happenings. That is why we have to be so careful and so expectant in dealing with the mystery of persons. For we are in the image of God, and flesh and blood is the way in which we get on to the infinite and the greatness of love and the infinity of love.

The world, for instance, is not anthropocentric (centred on man), as we now know. Once upon a time people seem to have thought that the world was centred on man, and they had a rather small view of the world. Now we have come to a more infinite view of the universe and we cannot suppose for one moment that the world of the universe is centred on us. Nothing in the universe is anthropocentric. But we are able to get on to the mysteries and patterns and possibilities of the whole universe. I am sure that this is why we are able to break genetic codes, why we are able to split the atom, why we have the power to enter into collaboration with the creativity of God and therefore have the power to destroy the creation. This is the other side of it. The cosmos side can become the chaos side. The very powers that we have can become self-destructive if they are turned in on ourselves and made selfish and self-regarding. But I am sure that we have these powers because it is not, again, a matter of mere metaphor that we are in the image of God. We have emerged out of what God has created, through God's always sustaining and for the purposes of God's promises, as material atoms which have come together eventually to be persons: persons being made for love, and therefore in the image of God, and able to collaborate with God. The reason why we human beings can map the universe or the universe of universes, the reason why we are able to break the genetic codes, why we have to make up our minds about whether or not we will make babies in test tubes, why we have questions about surrogate mothers and so on, is that actually we are in the image of God.

We can pick up everything about the universe – or at least we can grow more and more in the knowledge of the actual patterns and powers and possibilities of the universe – because we are in the image of God and the universe is theocentric. The universe is not centred on men, not centred on men and women, not centred on us; it is centred on God, because God made it, God is sustaining it, God is working out his infinitely promising purposes through it. But we are involved too. This is the mystery, the challenge and in some ways the terror; and I think we are seeing some of the terror now. If we could enter into this mystery of God the Holy Trinity I think we would see that we ought to be terrified by the abuse of our powers. But that very terror which God is putting upon us is in his loving purposes, that we may be so terrified by the abuse of our powers that we may repent individually, collectively, nationally and internationally, and bend these powers back, restore them to the very purposes which God has, which are those of always creating, always sustaining, always being promising. The universe is theocentric and we are in the image of God and therefore, infinitely small and apparently unimportant specks as we are (statistically neither you nor I count for anything in the number of molecules or the atoms or the energies of the universe), we are brought together in the image of God as persons who can love and respond and be free and therefore do wrong. So we are called actually to share in this great mystery of God, the great mystery of God's creation, the great mystery of God's sustaining, the great mystery of God's promise.

But how does this come down to earth? It comes down to earth, as far as we are concerned, in flesh and blood. That is why God was himself the Word Jesus. How can we cope with the greatness of this? Because God is still present as the Holy Spirit to pick us up into this and make us part of it. So the doctrine or the mystery of God the Holy Trinity is the Christian focussing of this understanding – in one way unbelievable and yet in another way under-

48

standable and infinitely exciting – that we are called to share in the sharing of God. This is in one sense literally true (although I am not sure that literal truth is of much interest to anybody; it gets rather dull! What really matters is much more symbolic truth and potential truth and actualizing truth and artistic truth and moral truth and personal truth and loving truth.) Every time we get tied down to the letter of something we probably miss the spirit of it, so we have to be careful about talking about literal truth. But we have to talk about real truth and the real truth, and the ultimate truth is of course God – who is the ultimate reality, who is therefore always promising as well as always creating. He is not going to be got down by any other reality; and if we think 'but the reality of chaos or the reality of sin and the reality of destruction is so great that it is difficult to believe in God', then we are confronted with God as Jesus Christ on the cross. Here is God in the midst of the very chaos, the very destruction, the very disobedience and the very distorting, and that is where he equally displays that he is God. So love is determined to deal with everything, and love is over-spilling in the Spirit to pick us up into all this.

Which leads me to my final point. You will notice in the diagram that while God is outside the world he is in block capitals and quite clear. But when he is inside the world he has to be broken up. We have the big God in the world in dotted letters. This is to indicate what is surely the experience of all the faithful through all the ages, which is that as we travel through this world there is no ultimate proof of the existence of God and no final guarantee in anything else that God exists. The reason is quite simple. He is God. Nothing could establish the existence of God other than God himself. For a thing can only establish the existence of that with which it is commensurate. It can point; it can promise; it can provoke; it can entice; it can give us glimpses – so that when we have been believing in God and then we feel totally depressed we may see a glimpse in the face of two human beings and say 'Ah, yes! That's right! Love is the ultimate power.' All the things that have been hinted to us are true.

Let me tell you a story about this. I was once in New York,

which can be a very depressing city, especially if you are on your own. I had been told by a television producer that if I was going to be an up-to-date purveyor of the gospel before I came back to him to help with a programme, I had to see some important films. So, being at that time an easily impressionable young man, I started going to films. I went to one late at night when I was in a hotel near Forty-Second Street, New York. It was extremely depressing, so I came out into the streets of New York where one is quite likely to be mugged, feeling not only depressed but also frightened and very much on my own. I was in Times Square and Forty-Second Street thinking to myself: 'The people who say that the world is hell and that we are degenerate and going down the drain rapidly are absolutely right, and I am not at all sure I can believe in God.' And as I was walking back to the hotel, looking over my shoulder in case someone should either mug me or run me down, I suddenly heard some disco music being played. Normally, I am not much impressed by disco music but welcoming any port in a storm, I went towards it. Standing in front of this dive were two of the ugliest people I have ever seen. One of the gifts New Yorkers seem to have is that they look ugly already, and then they wear spectacles and pork-pie hats which make them look even uglier! These two very ill-favoured people, a man and a woman, were hand in hand and dancing up and down, and they were obviously immensely enjoying one another. There was a sort of glow about them and a sort of smile. And the Lord said to me, 'There! You see. Anywhere I am my image is around. People can discover me through one another, so kindly go home and go to sleep peacefully and don't go around being a drip!' I could multiply that again and again.

The signs and the signals are there and our conviction is renewed and goes on, but doesn't prove it. There is no way of proving it, because it is so great and so glorious that it cannot be reduced to something which will be proved. If God is at the heart of things in Jesus Christ and his cross, there is, of course, further trouble here, for a struggle is going on. There is much in the world that undoubtedly counts against God. It is not easy to believe in God when you begin to enter into the real passion of

50

things, is it? It is not easy lightly to believe in God when you see, for instance, all the queues of disillusioned youths who seem to have no future at the moment. What is going on here? How can we believe in God, great and glorious as he is, in this sort of a world? So to believe in God is always to be challenged. There is no proof of God, and there would be much against God were it not for the fact that he is as he always was and always will be: the God who creates and comes, the God who sustains and cares, the God who promises and suffers; so that the assurance is built up again and again. Faith is built up again and again through experience; through sharing with others, through being called back, for instance, out of one's faithlessness by somebody who is being faithful, by being renewed. I must testify, feeble as what I say may be, that nearly every time I start to read the Bible, especially the Psalms and some of the great thoughts of St Paul or some meditative glimpse in the Synoptic Gospels, that some newness comes, something which speaks to one's condition in a manner which is only gift. Therefore I am obliged, and happy and renewed in being sure that the giver is there. The giver is there! But it cannot be proved and he is not our possession because he is so much greater.

Those who think that they possess God are possessed by something more like the devil! We cannot possess God, but God again and again possesses us. As Augustine says, every time we find him we find him because he has already found us. That is why discipleship, exploration, getting back to the basics and trying again and going deeper, is absolutely of the essence of knowing God and serving God and having faith in him. He cannot be pinned down and he will not be pinned down, but he is always creating, sustaining, promising, coming and therefore always to be discovered as being and always to be worshipped. And the more we remind one another of that calling and the more we seek to sustain one another in that calling, the more we shall be convicted by God, convinced of God, assured about God and then plunged back into the world to live in it for God where he is, so to speak, broken up by the world and broken up in the world but giving himself to us sufficiently for us to continue to witness to him, to continue to worship him and to continue to serve him. That is why after one has been seeking to investigate the mystery of God the Holy Trinity and has then focussed in on Jesus and his cross it is necessary to go on and consider the people of God and the Spirit, which brings us to us! For just as we are in the image of God, so it is we who are called to name God and witness to him in the world. And if, having read one or two things which seem to you to make some sense about this you look in the mirror and see what you actually look like and see into your own heart and then shake your head and say 'My God, no!' that is precisely the point. He has given himself to us as one of us to redeem us. So, the sky is the limit; and as the sky is the limit, we can get down to earth and get on with it.

5

Rediscovering the Truth about Jesus

In the previous chapter I suggested that one way of being clear about what Christian faith, life in the church, is all about was to say that it is about sharing in the sharing of God. The overflowing goodness and love and power of God has produced all the processes of creation, and the purpose of this overflowing is that God should share himself. In that connection I produced a diagram about God which made it clear that God comes at the beginning, because God is always creating, and that God comes at the end, because God is always promising. God came underneath the diagram because God is always sustaining, and God so to speak shot through the diagram because God is always sharing. Through the diagram I tried to make the point that though this world which was created by God has the promise of God in it, is sustained by God and is the field for the sharing of God, it is experienced as being quite as much chaos as cosmos. We do not live in the world, we are not able to handle the world for ourselves, in a manner which is wholly consistent with any understanding of God. There are anti-features; there are chaotic features; and there are absurd features, just as there are ordering features, loving features and hopeful and promising features. There is both chaos and cosmos. And I argued that there are all sorts of signs of God and signals from God to help us to get to know about him and to practise faith in him in the midst of this sort of world.

In the middle of the diagram of God and the world is a cross with words set round it: Jesus the Word. So in the middle of the chaos, the threats of chaos and the possibilities of cosmos, I set as central to our understanding of the world and our understanding of God the cross of Jesus, the Word of God. This is meant diagrammatically to indicate that we are Christians because we believe and are sure that Jesus and his cross are absolutely central to our knowledge of God, our practice of the presence of God and our hope of God.

How did that faith and conviction come about?

It seems to me that there are three basic points in our believing and trusting that Jesus is central to our knowledge of God.

1. God raised Jesus up.

2. That means that Jesus is the Messiah (the Greek for which is 'the Christ').

3. That means that the power of God's kingdom is suffering love and that the promise of God's kingdom is for all.

Let us look at these three points in rather more detail.

First, God raised Jesus up. It is absolutely clear that we should never have heard of the gospel of God, of the good news of God in Jesus, had it not been for the resurrection. In other words, had not the disillusioned disciples of Jesus of Nazareth met him after his death in a totally new way.

I think that it is essential to be clear about this, no matter what questions can be raised, and in other contexts indeed *need* to be raised, about the New Testament narratives.

Jesus of Nazareth aroused great expectations about the kingdom of God. He made a remarkable impact, which is witnessed to in various ways, especially in the Gospels. But above all he raised the great expectation that something really powerful and important about the kingdom of God was about to happen.

Then he was crucified, by a combination of the Roman civil authorities and the Jewish religious authorities. Here we should bear in mind – especially those of us who are deeply committed to religion and the Christian religion – that if we are to understand the Bible correctly we must note that the two authorities that turn out to be enemies of God are the government and the church. That is a point which I have already made in the previous chapter.

54

As a result Jesus was dead and buried, and the disciples and the women who had invested great hopes in him were shattered. That was that. Yet from the third day after his burial onwards this same Jesus of Nazareth was encountered by various disciples and various of the women. He was encountered as alive, encountered not as a ghost but as a person, a power and a presence who was in some real sense outside them and beyond them. He was encountered in such a way that they built up the conviction that this Jesus had not just *survived* death or *escaped* death; the only way in which they could put it was that he had been raised up by God so that death could no longer hold him. He was on the other side of death.

This was the assurance of the resurrection. It was this steady building up of dynamic conviction which turned the disciples into apostles. And this was part of a whole process which is subsequently told in the story of the descent of the Holy Spirit and the preaching of the gospel.

I think that it is very necessary to be clear that for the people who preached the gospel of the risen Jesus Christ, nothing could have been more real than their assurance of his resurrection, of his liveliness, of his abiding liveliness. It was so real that it made all the difference in the world. It was so real that it was more important than life itself. If you want to assess the *reality* of faith in the resurrection I suggest that you don't play around with particular details or particular facts, which can be explained one way or another, but that you pay attention to the effect that this belief had on turning disciples into apostles: on the preaching of the apostles and of the subsequent and *continuing* effect.

This effect is exemplified by a splendid story told of the aged Bishop Polycarp of Smyrna early in the second century when there was one of those bouts of persecution in which Christians got involved every so often. The Roman magistrate before whom Polycarp, who was clearly a very respected man, appeared, said to him (I paraphrase to make the point): 'Now look here, both you and I are educated men, we know that religion has its place in society; you mustn't get too worked up about it and above all you mustn't die for it. Why not burn a pinch of incense to the emperor

and reconcile that with your whole business about the Lord Jesus?'
But Polycarp retorted that he had served his Lord for seventy
years and could not deny him now. So Polycarp was put to death
because he felt it more important, more logical, more *real* to be
faithful to the Risen Lord, Jesus Christ, than to temporize with
the Lord Augustus, the lord emperor. That is the sort of reality
which the first Christians found, as subsequent Christians have
also found, in the resurrection. And that is the sort of reality
which is at the heart of faith in God, through Jesus Christ. It is
something which will face up to the most certain reality known to
us, which is the reality of death.

We have to be absolutely clear about the nature of this understanding which turned the disciples into the apostles: this faith,
this discovery, this conviction, this commitment that God had
raised Jesus up. The discovery of the Risen Lord, Jesus Christ, *was
not public*. That is to say, it was not something that anybody could
see or that convinced all who saw it and shared it. For as the
narratives themselves show, in any case not all were convinced (see
Matthew 28.17: 'they worshipped him, but some doubted'). And
clearly it was not a totally public declaration, because the first
Christians were a small sect. They then grew rapidly. But at no
time have any Christians been able to produce a public knock-
down argument about the resurrection of Jesus Christ. The perception of the resurrection, the conviction of the resurrection,
commitment to the resurrection and being saved by the resurrection is and always will be a matter of *faith*. But it is absolutely vital
to be clear that this does not make it less real: the question
involved is how we get on to the reality of God.

It is absolutely characteristic of God's dealings with men and
women that he risks faith and responsibility because, as far as I can
see, he is a God of love and therefore he is committed to freedom.
You cannot be *made* to love. You have to *learn* to love. You
cannot be *forced* into truth. You have to receive the truth and
respond to the truth. You cannot be part of responding to God by
a knock-down argument because that would be the work of a devil
who was determined to take you out of yourself in order to fulfil
yourself. Whereas God is determined to enable you to be yourself

56

in order to fulfil yourself. In a sense – why do you think he has bothered to create us? So, the freedom and the love is there, and if you study the New Testament carefully – certainly if you pursue the great traditions of spirituality in the Christian faith – you will find that there never is a knock-down argument, only a reality to which we may respond in freedom in faith. This seems to me to be central to God's dealing; and it is central to our understanding of the reality of the resurrection.

In view of certain controversies which have arisen around my name, it may be worth remarking in passing that this is why the question of a *physical* body in the resurrection is, strictly speaking, irrelevant. There is a summary statement about that in I Corinthians 15.35ff. The New English Bible translates the opening words of the passage: 'But, you may ask, How are the dead raised? In what kind of body? A senseless question?' That, though, is a polite rendering of what Paul actually said. He calls the question 'moronic'. Moron! Foolish! 'Thou fool,' is the rather more pungent and pointed translation in the Authorized Version. It is funny how modern translations try to take the edge off the Bible and make it slightly more polite. The Bible is full of disturbing and awkward remarks and we always seem to want to tone it down.

Paul's discussion goes on to talk about earthly bodies and spiritual bodies, but that is not the main point here. The main point is that the reality of the resurrection is quite clear and quite decisive, and it is what every Christian's faith is built on. But we have to leave the details, which can never be proved and will never be proveable, and we have to live the life. The whole of Christianity turns on the fact that God raised up Jesus. This is a certainty of faith, and we go on from there.

That brings us to a second point. That means that Jesus is the Messiah, and being the Messiah involves the cross. In a sense we Christians have become so familiar with the pattern of the Gospel narratives, the way in which they lead up to the passion, and the passion leads on the resurrection, and Good Friday is followed by Easter Day, that we have forgotten what a shattering discovery it was to see that Jesus was the Messiah and that the Messiah is the crucified one. But we need to recover that sense in order to rediscover faith.

The discovery was shattering because the Messiah was the one who was to bring in the kingdom of God, and one would naturally suppose that the kingdom of God is brought in by power and triumph and visible victory. But in fact, according to us Christians, the Messiah turned out to be Jesus and we discovered this by the resurrection of Jesus from the dead after his death on the cross. This means that it is Jesus who is God's way of being and doing towards us. Christians have never yet lived up to that. That is another reason why we are going to need eternity to live into, for the Messiah brings in God's kingdom, and the kingdom is where God shares himself without interruption or distortion. As in the Lord's Prayer, if God's name were really hallowed and if his will was done on earth as in heaven, then his kingdom would have come – there would be no interruption to the love of God: God would be shared with everybody and everything without interruption. The kingdom is where God's love totally rules. This is what we long for, this is what we pray for, and this is what we are asked to work for. But so far it has never come off fully, except in and as Jesus. Jesus is the Messiah, Jesus is where God's kingdom comes; Jesus is where the love of God is totally uninterrupted and fulfilled. So it is Jesus who brings in the kingdom by being God's way of being and doing as far as we are concerned. Everything that contradicts the kingdom – sin, disobedience, destruction, death – is dealt with by the suffering of Jesus, the identification of Jesus and the death of Jesus. God is at one with us; Love is triumphing by taking it all on, for the crucified is the Messiah.

It is extremely difficult to enter into all this, but it is absolutely essential because – to put in a personal word at this point – it is because of this that it seems to *me* personally possible to believe and hope in God in a world like this. There are so many things in the world which seem to contradict the possibility of a God who is love. Famine in Ethiopia, the obscenity of the arms race, the misery in something like the Miners' Strike with all the confusion in it – how can there actually be a loving God in a world like this? Now it seems to me that one can believe that above all because *the* agent and *the* Word and *the* revelation of God is a crucified man, a man who has indicated that love deals with these problems by suffering: that is the way love fights. Being the Messiah involves the cross. And there is no way of rediscovering faith in Jesus without being in some way open to all this reality of suffering. This is the way God goes, this is the way love triumphs, this is precisely why love cannot be defeated.

As we know, if we are up against something, we get angry, we respond in anger; if someone fights us, we fight back. That leads to more trouble, and it goes on and on. If it were possible and if we could be part of this way of absorbing love, of love absorbing everything, to the degree that we can get grace from God to enter into the soft answer that turns away wrath, then we shall be part of that which, I think, one can quite clearly and reasonably see, is actually undefeatable. A love which can suffer everything is quite clearly indestructible. There, it seems to me, is the centre of hope.

So the crucified Lord is the Lord and God's Christ. That means, thirdly that, as I have already indicated, the power of God's kingdom is suffering love and the promise of God's kingdom is for all. But what is at work in the purpose of God, by the expression of God, for the promise of God, is this suffering love which absorbs, enters into, endures and comes up triumphant. Things are not finally sorted out by triumphalistic and knock-down power. Of course that sort of power can win in the temporary measures of this life, like running governments, sustaining states, keeping local societies going, and even in the problems of families. A cartoon I saw which pretended to be about God had a picture of God sitting on a cloud looking very cross and saying: 'You love one another, or I'll come down there and thump you all.' But that is not God, nor is it his ultimate and final and real way. Growth for peace, growth for eternity, ultimately comes from suffering, absorbtion, identification. This is the only way, and in the end it is the inevitable way: that which is basic to true faith and hope and love. That also means that the promise of God's kingdom is for all, something which we find Paul wrestling with on the basis of his discovery of the crucified Messiah.

If God is this sort of loving, identifying, absorbing God, then he does not depend on people observing particular laws or indeed needing to have particular forms of religion to be rightly related to him. He is concerned to love them into a relationship with him no matter what they do. There is no special choice or special religion here: the crucified Messiah makes it clear that God is for all. Power and self-righteousness are not the way to serve God, but love and suffering and death, and that means that everyone is invited to be included and can be included. And that is why Christians have to be reminded again and again when they are rediscovering faith about Jesus that we have a universal mission. We are not called out by God solely for our own comfort (though it is immensely for our own comfort, salvation and eternity). Our calling is not a particular calling to come into a comfortable huddle, as it were, and be grateful that God has chosen *us*, and then turn our backs on the world, or cherish our cultic religion so that it is not disturbed by the world, because it is the God of the whole world who has been Christ Jesus, who has given himself in love, so that the mission is universal. As the New Testament puts it: this is for all the nations. The New Testament repeats that again and again: it is for all.

Every time the Christian church settles down and thinks that it has somehow staked out its own claim to divine territory and human territory, it has to be broken up and sent out again. At present, for instance, we are being made to think again about various aspects of something that Paul said long ago: that in Christ there is neither Jew nor Greek, bond nor free, male nor female. We have to work that out again with regard to racism, with regard to the oppressed and the people who are on top and, of course, with regard to male and female. Many people find all these challenges very frightening, but the dynamic, the faith of Christians, who see God in Jesus Christ, is that this is for all. The understanding must continually be universalized. It is essential to keep on fighting against the boundaries in the name of love, which wants to save us all and build us all up.

All this also means that we Christians in the church have to face the constant criticism by God of religious exclusiveness and self-righteousness. If God is as he is in Jesus, if Jesus is the Messiah,

60

the crucified Messiah, the God at one with us, then the whole basis of the relationship with God is forgiveness. And the way you enter into forgiveness is first of all by being forgiven. It is when we know that we are forgiven – and it is we who are the primary sinners, we who are dependent upon God – that we are set free for this universal mission.

Therefore this understanding of God in Christ Jesus whom he has raised, as the dying and risen Messiah, pushes us into this understanding of love and universal mission. I think that that makes clear something which I touched on earlier: there is a very real sense in which the God and Father of our Lord Jesus Christ is against religion. His only interest in religion is presumably his interest in any other human affairs, that the practice should put people in touch with him and should set them free to serve their neighbour. And anyone who uses, any group which uses, religion for exclusive purposes, for their own satisfaction, for moralistic purposes which exclude people, is simply being an enemy of God.

At this point one of the great enemies is solemnity. We must not be solemn about ourselves or our sins. They have to be taken seriously, but once we take them solemnly we are trapped, whereas the whole object is to be set free: for God, people and the world. Jesus shows us that God is for all, for love, for freedom, and so our faith and our hope is in him. The following of the risen Christ, the understanding of the resurrection, the practice of the gospel, is involved in becoming part of this believing people and then going on. That is why in the next chapter we shall go on to people. For the question which faces us at this point is how we live out the life of the Spirit, which is the Spirit of Jesus Christ coming from God to enable us to be people in relation to God.

61

6

Rediscovering the Truth about People

Looking into the mystery of God and thinking about the truth about Jesus brings us to the issue of the truth about people. It is possible to produce diagrams about the mystery of God, the Holy Trinity; it is possible to talk at length of the truth about Jesus; but where does all this come down to earth? The answer is that it comes down to earth in people.

God comes down to earth supremely in Jesus. And Jesus shows that this glorious, holy and mysterious God is committed to people in a down-to-earth way. It must follow, therefore, that if we are getting glimpses of the truth about God, the truth about God which is in Jesus Christ, the truth which we certainly want to be living out in the Holy Spirit and in the church, it must be something which comes down to earth to do with people. Because God is committed to people in a down-to-earth way. That doesn't mean that God is confined to down-to-earthness or that God is only met in people. Nor does it mean, as we shall see in due course, that everything you meet in people is to do with God. But it is a focal point of Christianity that God is in people, God as one of us.

And that leads into a second point. People is us. We are people. Being mixed up with people or putting up with people or trying to get away from people is where we start from. And it is where I start from. If we believe in this great and holy and glorious God who is the down-to-earth God, then paying attention to me, to us, to where we are, is a necessary and absolutely essential part of being more in touch with God, getting more on to what he is about and what he wants us to do. It therefore seems to me proper and indeed necessary that in this exploration into rediscovering the truth we should come to the business of people.

Since what we are doing can rightly be called reflection, we might start by thinking of looking in a mirror. Suppose you look in a mirror and gaze fairly intently for a bit. Who are you looking at? Think about it for a moment. And then reflect a little more. Not about anything in particular; just think. When you do come to think of it, it is very odd that you can think, especially that you can think about yourself.

When you come to think of it, the business of being somebody who is aware of being somebody has something mysterious about it. And when you go on to think about it you will see that whatever is mysterious about it – and the very fact that I can think of me being me – actually depends on other people having treated you as yourself (having talked to you, and so on). Talking and listening is a way of giving and picking up signs, and how people pick up signs, how they develop, is also a mysterious business. To go back to the mirror: you can not only think about yourself, but you can also ask yourself: 'Who does my wife, or my husband, or my brother or my sister or my friends see when they look at me?' Then you are getting on to something interesting.

Look at somebody whom you yourself know well and love a lot. Sometimes you may not have a clue about them; you may have no idea what is really going on in their heads. Sometimes I get that dreadful feeling even about my wife, after thirty-five years of marriage. But the other way round, sometimes my wife seems to know what I am going to be thinking even before I have started to think it. Sometimes you are right inside people and sometimes you are just not there. It seems to me that one can't be at all sure: there is mystery. It is a mystery which sometimes has a great deal of loneliness in it but on the other hand sometimes has a great deal of longing in it – and then it has something quite marvellous in it – you are just there together. You don't have to think about it at all.

And then, of course, if you go on from there and look at what we actually do to one another, it is sometimes mysterious or marvellous, and sometimes quite awful. So the mystery – or the muddle – builds up. And then you come to the one thing that is certain: I shall die – and that is a feeling which builds up as you get older.

So what could be the truth about people who are like you or me? Is it all a tragedy that comes to nothing much, or a piece of nonsense? Here another consideration surely comes in: isn't it all a matter of chemistry and genes anyway?

I had a most uncomfortable encounter with that question after I had been ordained deacon. My mother was at the service in the morning, and then she came to my 'do' in the evening and I was preaching. We drove home in the car and she said to me, 'Well, dear, all the time you were preaching I was thinking how when you were quite small you used to line up the chairs and preach to them.' There was I, thinking that I had had a call to preach, that I had responded to God, that I had been through selection for ordination and theological college, but it wasn't anything to do with that at all: it had been built into my genes from the beginning. It was predetermined. My mother knew all about it. She encouraged me to think that I was doing heroic things while she knew that I was just working out the inevitable and hoping that I wouldn't bore too many people!

There's something in it: the matter of genes and chemistry. You realize that especially if you have friends who are psychiatrists, as I do. For example, I had a colleague once who had very acute ups and downs. And when he had downs you just had to rally round and put up with him; sometimes he had to have time off. Then he had various tests and it proved that he had a biochemical problem which carefully arranged doses of a drug dealt with. A matter of pure biochemistry – not will control or anything like that – enabled him to be much more steadily what I think one would call himself. We are very bodily after all. So does that mean that everything is fixed?

Are we a mystery, a puzzle, or just a piece of nonsense? This, I think, is perhaps where God, who is as he is in Jesus, comes in.

64

The Christian claim, the Christian understanding based on the Bible, on faith, on tradition and on practice, is that we can take this mystery very seriously. We can say quite rightly how odd it is that chemicals, when they get organized into people, can actually think, love, suffer and hurt one another. We can follow up the clue that it takes other people to enable people to be people, or even themselves. You can't become anybody if nobody talks to you. We have various things at our disposal which, if they are used in a disciplined, loving and understanding way, can set people free from what would otherwise trap them in most dreadful moods and horrors. But it depends on somebody else that this should be done. There are clues here, and they are all to be understood as being clustered round the notion of the image of God.

You and I are in the image of God. That is not a claim that everything is centred on us and that to be in the image of God means that we are on the throne of the universe and everything depends on us. It is to say that the great mystery, which has to be understood in a down-to-earth way and yet points up to heaven, glory, eternity and infinity, is that each of us, who have in a way emerged out of chemicals and so far as our bodily make-up is concerned will return to chemicals is so constructed that we can get on to God's wavelength. That is because the whole universe is actually on God's wavelength. He is the creator and maker of all things, the power behind all things and the presence which sustains all things, the promise to whom all things point. And it is because we are in that image that small, insignificant, temporary, frail, fragile as we are, we can actually get on to the truth about the universe.

To the mysteries that I have been trying to discuss from inside can be added the absolutely amazing mystery of what the human mind and the human spirit is capable of. I do not think that it is just accidental that human beings can get so organized that they can plumb the universe both microscopically and macroscopically, beyond anything that we can imagine and in a way we can only put down in figures. All this is evidence that we are indeed, as the Bible claims and as the Christian faith holds, in the image of God, able to resonate to God and to be on God's wavelength.

In that perspective, rediscovering the truth about people involves at least the following.

First rediscovering the truth about people is rediscovering that they are persons. It is worth reflecting on this notion of 'people' as 'persons', because the notion of 'persons' points especially to relationships. People are lively and loving human beings in relationships which stretch as far as God. One way of defining or pointing to a very important truth about people is to say that people are what their relationships enable them to become. That is not necessarily an encouraging remark; it can be very depressing. For people who do not have good personal relationships do not develop into good persons and so there is a knock-on effect. One of the reasons why we have so much vandalism and trouble is because for some reason or other relationships have broken down in a big way.

Men and women are what their relationships enable them to become. So the whole business of building up persons is to do with building up relationships, and if one wants to know more about God, as the First Epistle of John reminds us, if we don't love the brother whom we have seen, how can we say that we love God whom we have not seen? If we can't start building up relationships here, how can we talk about relationships with God?

But potential relationships do spread as far as God, so anyone who has a theory about people or treats people as if they were less than persons who are not only capable of being related to one another but are actually meant to be related to God is making a very serious mistake. That is the main reason for being very careful with people who want to reduce human beings either to citizens or to members of certain classes, or to those of a certain biological or psychological or medical category. People have to be categorized in certain circumstances in order to be dealt with, but the categories into which they are put is never the final truth about them. There is always more to it.

We must also remember that *all* people are persons. That means that in the sight of God all have equal potentiality. That has important implications for much that troubles us in our society at present, as for example the relationship between men and women.

What does it mean to treat men and women as being equally persons? We don't quite know. For instance, should we ordain women or not? Some people think that we should not and some people think that we should. (But that is really only a private and in some ways a church matter which we shall have to tackle in the light of all sorts of other questions which come up in connection with changes in our society over the relationship between men and women.)

In many parts of the country there is a problem as to whether white people, black people and, say, yellow people are all equally persons. That is what is behind racism: not some special sin, but just ordinary problems about how one treats people who are different. So perhaps the central challenge in rediscovering the truth about people as persons is to realize that *all* people are persons, especially those who are different from us. And probably for the sake of our personalities we actually need to receive from people who are different from us things about them as persons. But that is going to take a good deal of working out.

This brings me to a second point. While it is true that all people are persons, if we are to be realistic and down-to-earth we have to face the fact that all people are also obstacles, or what in theological language is called sinners. It is no good going on romantically about people as persons, and people in the image of God, when one thinks of what they actually *do*. People are liable to use the very things that make us persons as things that actually spoil other people as persons. You wouldn't be a person if you weren't a self, and you wouldn't be a self if you didn't have motivation and direction and wanted to get somewhere, but again and again the way you actually use your motivation, your self, is to come up against other selves. After all, to be a person is to be a self, and yet very often you exercise yourself in such a way that you are being selfish.

Now while being selfish goes with self, it doesn't actually promote selves. This is one of the problems, which spills off in all sorts of directions. For instance, if you don't motivate people you will never get anything done, but if you don't enable them to make a profit, how will you motivate them? And if they make too much of a profit they will spoil other selves – so what do you do about it? That is a real problem all the time.

All people are obstacles and sinners. That applies to *everybody*; it isn't only the other people who are the obstacles and sinners. That is the truth that we have to be constantly rediscovering. That is why we have confession every time we go to church on Sunday, and it isn't just a routine matter. It is actually something much more profound. It is facing up to the fact that, mysterious, baffling and confusing as it is, something has gone wrong – it is called the fall in biblical language, in picture language.

We have to reckon with the way in which it is true that all people are obstacles and sinners, just as it is true that all people are persons. Among other things, that means that if we are going to be part of rediscovering the truth about people we simply have to learn the truth about ourselves, which is that the whole matter of needing to be forgiven for being a sinner actually starts with us. And it is only as we learn *that* that we shall be in a position to be used by God to remind other people of their sins. So often we try to dodge the issue by telling other people off about their sins; we are far better at spotting other people's sins than our own. But it is important for us to build into our lives and into the lives of other people an understanding that *we* are as much obstacles and sinners as anyone else, but are not deterred by this because we know that God judges us as sinners to save us. He is drawing attention to this reality to get us out of it, not to keep us under. And that leads to a third point.

We have to rediscover the truth about people not only as obstacles but as resources: for the building up of one another for the kingdom of God. For what is at the heart of Christianity, as Paul tells us in Romans 6.14, is that sin will not have dominion over us. That is just one way of pointing to the truth of God as it is in Jesus at the heart of things, the truth that God himself has involved himself in this 'obstacle-ness', in this sinfulness, and has done whatever needs to be done in order to make it clear that being an obstacle doesn't have the last word; being a sinner doesn't have the last word; being somebody who spoils other people and oneself doesn't have the last word. It is God in his love who has the last word. Therefore people are *always* to be considered not first as sinners – that is only something that we have to go through – but first as persons with infinite possibilities of relationships, and then as resources.

The rediscovery of people as resources seems to me to be particularly important in the present situation in our society. The way our society is organized – and I think that we are in a betwixt-and-between stage where one sort of society has nearly run down and we are now having to learn how to be another sort of society – is actually having the effect of making more and more people look as if they are not resources, that society has no use for them. We have all been dominated by the notion that what really makes a person important is his or her job, and what he or she gets paid for it. So that when we move into a phase when literally millions of people can in a sense have no job, it looks as if they are not resources and have no worth. So the rediscovery of the truth that people are resources seems to me to come very near to the heart of working out what down-to-earth faith about God is really about.

It also gives us the encouragement of knowing that people are the very best resources we have, no matter what conditions we have to live under. A consumer society in which it looked as if what were called 'standards of living' could go on going up seems to have bamboozled us into believing that people can only enjoy themselves, be enjoyable, and share life with one another if they have a whole lot of other things on top of that. Now I would be the last to think that we ought to be against spending power; it doesn't seem to me that we should go into a sort of total Puritan decline and say that it is a good thing that people can no longer afford washing machines, so we can get back to the sink and slavery. But we do need to re-learn something which simpler societies, primitive societies and others, have known and we seem to have lost, that it is people who are the basic resources. One can find a terrific lot in life from and through people. In my various travels around the world for the World Council of Churches I found that people who seemed to have absolutely no prospects, living in difficult political situations and in poverty, were grouping together and living lives of what one could only call joy. They weren't all happy, and it wasn't always very enjoyable, but they were helping one another to make sense of their lives and finding immense resources in one another.

How that applies to us in this rather betwixt-and-between stage is something that needs to be worked out. But what I have just said is an important part of a lesson which we have to relearn. Or perhaps it is that we have to learn a new lesson. For it also seems to me to be true that we are at a stage when we actually have to *grow* a new society. We can't invent it. Perhaps that is why politics is in such a muddle at the moment.

This is not a lesson that can be stumbled on in five minutes or invented by some new bit of political insight, although we do need new political insights. We do *know*, and have every reason for believing, that people are in the image of God. And that means us. We do *know*, and we have every reason for believing, that people are persons, *all of them*, and especially the ones who are different. Of course we know that people are sinners and there are plenty of obstacles, but we also know that sin shall not have dominion over us, so there must be ways of finding how people are resources. And that must be done, finally, in relation to the overall belief that people are meant to be heirs to the kingdom. There is always more to people and there is always more promised to people, and we are in the business of helping ourselves and others to discover that we are on the way to this kingdom of God, this fullness where relationships will be fulfilled. We are to set up examples of sharing and enjoyment of sharing and signs of the greater sharing which is offered us in the end. Now we get only glimpses; and now we only have the chance to offer glimpses to other people. But the hope is that these will be fulfilled in the kingdom of God. And it is never to be forgotten that that is what we are destined for. Even when we do forget and treat people as less than in the image of God, we need to recall that image. We need to insist on it again and again in ordinary matters in our society and be ready to stand up for it, even if we do not have the physical resources and the other resources to treat people as we would like to. That is at least how we can show that we are on the way to the kingdom.

Worshipping God the Holy Trinity, and living by faith through

Jesus Christ, means receiving grace to live out the knowledge that nobody can be fully a person until other people are fully persons. I cannot be fully me until you are fully you, and that means that you must be you in such a way that it enables me to be me; and similarly I must be me in such a way that it enables you to be you.

I think that this is actually, literally true. It picks up the two points that I made right at the beginning: that we are dependent on one another for being ourselves and that the work of the Holy Spirit and the offer that is made in Jesus Christ provide the possibility of sharing in the life of God and therefore sharing in the life of the Holy Trinity.

I know from my family life and also from my collaborative life at certain stages that I simply cannot do my job without other people. I have discovered again and again that if you collaborate with people and if you share with people, you personally discover things which you would never have discovered alone, and they discover things that they would never have discovered alone. There is much more to each of us because we are together. And it is quite clear to me that I would have no chance of being me, even as I am, without other people. So it is true that I cannot be fully me until you are fully you. I think that one of the exciting things about the possibilities of eternal life, as I have mentioned before, is that this means that we have the chance, eventually, of sharing in everything that anyone has ever discovered about life and goodness.

Another way of talking about this is to call it the reciprocity of love. In the end, if you *really* love, and if you are really set free to love, then you are not compelled to love but you can't help it. That is actually what you want to do above all. In another way, you can say that it is what above all you must do. But of course if what you *want* to do you *must* do, and if you must do it, so you want to do it, you are really being free by being you – or me, as the case might be.

We can think about this in different ways, and it actually comes down to earth in very practical ways, because we simply have to keep trying to learn as we go along. How can I be more me so that I am part of other people being more them? What needs to be changed so that more of them enables each one of them and me to be more me? We are really bound up in one another. And through this and in this there is the whole excitement of discovering the very love of God. That is what God is about – as I said right at the beginning. We are involved in sharing in the sharing of God, and I think that the way we share in the sharing of God is by rediscovering the truth about people.

7

Rediscovering the Truth about the Holy Spirit and the Church

If Christians are to develop as Christians, both in their own discipleship and in involvement with God and the purposes of God in this world, in the sort of intellectual, cultural, political and social situation of our time, then it is absolutely essential that every Christian who cares about being a Christian should be able to answer for herself or himself. As the First Epistle of Peter puts it, we must be able to give an account of the faith that is in us. It is essential that each Christian (as well as Christians in groups and congregations or larger aggregations or conglomerations of Christians) should have some answer which he or she has worked out personally, even if we are not very good at expressing it or cannot put it very well though we know it well enough inside ourselves, or even if we do not find it easy to share with others.

It is not a question of being able to give something like the 'right answers' to whatever the questions are, but saying what this or that aspect of Christianity means to one so far. The older I get, the clearer I am that in a way there are no 'right answers': only answers which have picked up some right echoes and begin to point in the right direction. After that we must rely on God to fill them out and change them as they go along.

Rather than having some encapsulated 'right answers', it is much more a question of making a living response to a living God amidst a group of other people who are seeking to live into this God, as well as out of this God: to live by love, towards love, to hope for love. It is much more a question of a living exploration and a living faith. And if we are to get on with that we have to be able, from time to time, simply to say what the faith means to us where we are, and to share this with other people. It is quite clear to me that unless people are able to do that, then the mission of the church will increasingly fade away. Mind you, if it fades away in this country, so much the worse for us. God will raise up the church elsewhere.

I am not bothered about the future of the church in the long run because God is God and has called the church into being; he will renew it whenever he wants to. I am, however, deeply concerned by the extent to which people in this country who belong to churches still take them for granted, and to an even greater extent are always looking backwards for meaning. If they can give any account at all they tend to do it in what you might call 'formula-like phrases'. For instance, they just repeat biblical phrases. The number of people who quote the Bible and have clearly never read it is very distressing. Or there are people who simply do not read the Bible but take little chunks out of it as if they were mantras or spells which can be repeated and will exorcise things like fear of death.

Actually, the Bible is the record of a set of responses which grew up over a very long time as a lot of people wrestled with life. We can see there how each in their day, they wrestle with life as it is to them and have something to say about it: about the way God encounters them as they continue in the tradition of the people of God, as they are encountering some crisis in their life or in the life of the nation, and therefore have to give an account of what God means to them at that moment. They talk about what it is to be a member of the house of Israel; what it is to have some hope of the kingdom of God; what it is to be convinced that Jesus is the Christ. In that tradition, I hope that what I too have been trying to do in these explorations has been to put before you an example of wrestling with questions today, in the world of today, about the faith into which we are called. I have been trying to show how we work out for ourselves in our time what we would say.

If we are going to be living disciples of a living faith to do with

74

the living God in the sort of world we have now, we must be able to put part of that faith, where we hook on to it, into our own words. And that also applies when we come to talk about the church. It is all very well having all sorts of theories about the church, but they have to be articulated. Some people derive one set of answers from their theories about the church, say to the question whether women should be ordained, while others derive a completely different set of answers from their theories. In all this, behind the theories, below the language of the theories, or alongside the language of the theories, we can see how they emerge – have to emerge – into ordinary language.

But now to the question of the church. What is the church, and where does it come from? My answer would be that 'it is the group of all groups who know themselves to be called to be in continuity and communion with the original group'.

I do not think that there is a theological word in that, with the possible exception of communion, but that is an ordinary sort of word. What I have said gives, I think, a description of what is meant – or ought to be meant – by a term like apostolicity: 'The group of all groups in continuity with the original group'. For what actually started the church? The nearest thing we seem to have to a historical hard fact is that a group of persons discovered that Jesus was the Christ. *This* Jesus. Not any Jesus, but the particular Jesus of Nazareth who is witnessed to in the Gospels; the particular Jesus of Nazareth who was crucified under Pontius Pilate and the particular Jesus of Nazareth whom, this group discovered, God had raised up. Whether they were right, what they really discovered, what it was that led them to discover it are all questions that can be, and are, discussed. But as a simple matter of fact it is the coming into being of this group who discovered that this Jesus is the Messiah, Christ, and therefore Lord and Son of God, which marks the beginning of the church.

The *World Christian Encyclopaedia*, published a few years ago, contained a most amazing statistical summary which indicated that there are something like ten main traditions of Christianity, divided into one hundred and fifty three main churches which break down into more than two thousand denominations. So who are Christians, what is 'the' church? If you feel bewildered by it all, something quite simple such as 'it is the group of all groups who want to be in continuity with the original group' both gives us something to hang on to and also a working definition. It is also, as I shall try to show, of practical relevance to the life of individual churches or congregations, no matter how they understand the doctrine of the church. As we have seen, the statement is all about apostolicity: the church, in a very simple historical sense of the term, is caused by Jesus and the discoveries about Jesus which we believe to be brought about by the Holy Spirit. Jesus Christ and the Holy Spirit are, as we have seen, one with the Father, so the church is connected with the Trinity and what the previous three chapters have been about.

What we have to do is to seek to be focussed where the original group was focussed, which is in discovering that Jesus is central to God's purpose, to God's being and to what God is doing. The church goes on because God goes on evoking this sort of faith: in God, through Jesus, in the Spirit. No matter what we are involved in, which might for example be discussing proposals about baptism, ministry and eucharist, or considering the suggestions made by the Anglican and Roman Catholic International Commission, what we must really be doing is to respond to God in Jesus through the Spirit as the first group responded to him. As I said earlier, had there not been a group which was convinced that Jesus was God's Christ, there would be no church. So if we are to go into matters about the church, we have to relate this to our understanding of Jesus as the Christ.

It is also important to remember that the church has an eternal and future dimension. When we talk about the communion of saints and life everlasting we are also talking about the church. It is necessary to put that in when we are trying to be simple in order to make it clear that the simplicity has something like 'an eternal dimension'.

So far we have been considering where the church comes from. Now we need to go on to ask: 'What does the church exist for?' My short answer to that is: 'To celebrate and promote worth in the name of God the Holy Trinity.' This introduction of the notion of worth, which is deliberately related to the notion of worship (the worship of God is to do with the worth-ship of God, and the worth which he is, offers and promises) follows on from the trains of thought leading through the three previous explorations. In talking about God, Jesus or people, one comes to the matter of worth, for God in and as Jesus Christ declares that people matter in an amazing and extraordinary way. What Christianity is really talking about is the quite extraordinary worth that God has invested in his concern for human beings, which he must see in human beings, what he hopes for from human beings and what he offers to human beings. Worth is what God sees in us. ('Herein was love – not that we loved God, but that he loved us.') Worth is what God offers to us. He is actually and practically, in a down-to-earth way, offering us a share in his life of eternity. So it is literally true that we are of infinite worth. That is not just a sort of metaphorical way of talking about how much it means to me to be me and how I would like to go on being me for ever. The worth that God offers us is the worth of sharing love with other loving and living people which can go on infinitely developing and multiplying into the infinity of God. This is the worth that God entices from us: powers beyond our own powers, possibilities that we had never dreamt of and an exceeding great weight of glory that we have only just begun to glimpse. This is the worth that God is determined to share with us by loving us through sin and death. That is the good news. That is what the gospel is about, and that is why the gospel involves the cross and salvation. God has committed himself to overcoming everything that is contrary to worth. Jesus in his resurrection and in the giving of his Spirit is showing that God is committed to paying all the costs of putting things right and getting on with the rightness. This is part of what lies behind the talk of atonement. We may turn the theories of the atonement into something literal and get into complications, but their dynamic impact is quite clear: God is investing himself in making us so worthwhile. That is why the Holy Spirit and the church have to go together – and if all this is more than we can take in, we have to be taken in by it. The church and the Holy Spirit cannot be separated: unless God himself is at work inside us and between us to develop our understanding of worth in this way, we cannot achieve anything.

A Roman Catholic theologian remarked that 'It is in the power of Jesus' Spirit that the church mediates God's concern for all men.' That is something worth remembering next time you have to cope with a leaking church roof! The reason why we are trying to keep things going is so that we can, in the power of Jesus' spirit, mediate God's concern for all men. We are not trying to keep the show going so that we can have a cosy place in which to come together on Sunday, a place in which we, our fathers and our grandfathers have been (although it is worth doing that because that is a sign of God's concern). We are not keeping the church on because it is our church and we would not dream of joining up with the people down the road, because after all their church is different and they have always had their Church Fayre on different days. We are keeping the church going so that we can mediate God's concern for all men and women and mediate this under-standing of God's concern in ways which take people's worth into account. How do we produce neighbourly sacraments of the down-to-earth of God so that we are mediating concern for all men and women? That is the question we have to ask.

Such a question puts all our activities in perspective. The first thing about the perspective is that it is godly; it must be to do with God, his infinite love and amazing worth. It is because it is about God that it is about good news and salvation. For if we are to promote the worth of all as God has invested himself in it, as he has committed himself to it, shown himself with it and for it in Jesus Christ, then of course we have to be saved. We and all men and women have to be saved from all unworthiness. That is why we are obliged to combat sin. Life and love have to confront sin.

If we are promoting worth, then we are fighting unworthiness. To put it in biblical terms, the love of God and the anger or wrath of God are one and the same thing. For if God is lovingly com-mitted to the total worth of his creatures, his love will be burn-ingly against everything that is unworthy.

While I was on holiday I had a little revelation. I saw in a church a picture of the Trinity over the main arch; it was simply three

78

interlocking circles. The top circle had fingers in blessing pointing down (that is, God offering his blessing, his worth, his love). One of the bottom circles had a cross (standing for Jesus, the way in which God has invested himself passionately in the world in order to redeem us, so that this blessing of worth can indeed overcome unworthiness). In the other circle there was a flame (which is the Spirit going up again). As the blessing of God is given to us through the forgiveness and love of Jesus Christ, so we are caught up into this flame of love, and the whole thing flames back into the blessing of God, and is to become love, blessing, worth and glory. That is the good news. But as I was sitting there in the church, on my own, looking at the picture, something clicked. It was one of those times when pictures suddenly look different from the way you have seen them before. The fingers were suddenly pointing in such a way as to say: *you* are under judgment; *you* can build up butter mountains when all those other people are starving; *you* can talk about the church when you argue about all those trivial things. Then I suddenly saw that the cross said: you know that you ought to be crossed out for the sort of things you are doing; there are endless things in you which need to be contradicted. And I saw what a flame does. It can actually cauterize. We will be saved, as Paul says, but so as by fire. The picture conveyed judgment, not blessing, and I really wanted to get out of church. But then I thought to myself: that is the point. In this sort of world, the sort of people we are, with the mystery of iniquity as well as the mystery of glory, love must also be judgment.

Love is against unworthiness for the sake of worth. So we must be quite clear that the perspective in which our activities are put, our gospel, is about godliness and salvation, about the worth of all, but does include the whole business of saving people from unworthiness so that we are committed to the confrontation between love and sin. We must never forget this, or the fact that it is directed at us in the first place, before we can be part of pointing it outwards.

A good deal of conflict among Christians is heightened by the uncertainties of the world around us. When a group of persons finds it difficult to advance their cause they are liable to start quarrelling amongst themselves over what the cause really is. This is a sort of displacement activity. Thus quite a lot of Christians suddenly decide that they will defend the faith by declaring that there is only one way of interpreting the resurrection or only one way of showing a spiritual gift or only one way of carrying on the church. Then they can start fighting other Christians, and it looks as if they can win victories – they do not have the nerve to go in for the really difficult battle, which is to spread the gospel. I think that much Christian quarrelling is a diversion. We do not have the nerve to go out into the world and wrestle as we should.

In this connection it is very important to be clear that being the church – if it comes from where it does and is concerned, as I suggest, with worth – will in fact involve a great variety and plurality and much experimentation in the life of the churches and our discipleship. In practice there is no one pattern of being the church, no one way of preaching the gospel and no one way or prompting worth and of fighting unworthiness. There is a whole set of ways which stem from the basic understanding and point in the final direction, which is the love and worth of God, but we must get used to the many ministries and gifts. We can waste too much time on internal controversy which diverts us from getting on in a variety of ways with being the church and serving people.

It is not a question of serving God in his way. Jesus Christ did that, but we cannot. It is a question of serving God in our way, in our various ways, which he will correct, forgive, bless and use. This needs to be worked out very practically. When we get worried that other people's varieties or ways of doing things are a wandering away from the faith instead of being faithful, then we should ask ourselves this question. 'Is this likely to be faithful to God in Christ?' in terms of the two questions: Where does the church come from? What does the church exist for? Can we give an account to one another of our varieties of serving God, of our differences in being the church, of our plurality of experiment with regard to our preaching the gospel? Can we tell other people how it is related to where the church comes from? This is what is involved in explaining how what we are doing, in our understanding responsibly under God, relates to scripture and tradition.

One part of the task of Christians in working out what varieties are permissible is for them to give an account to one another of how they understand what they are doing in relation to the tradition. Another very important part is to explain why we see what we are doing as having a real relationship to what the church is for. There has been far too much discussion in ecumenical circles and theology about whether we are in accordance with what the church comes from, and we forget the other question: are we in accordance with what the church is for? For the history of the church shows horrible abuses. Catholics can make a horrible abuse of Catholicism, even to the point of burning people. Protestants can make a horrible abuse of Protestantism, even – as a matter of fact – to burning people. Charismatics can make a horrible abuse of their charismatic authority and so dominate people that it drives them mad. Through the history of the church it is quite clear that every understanding of the church can be used for dominance, for power and for selfishness. So any sort of theologizing about what the church is for and whether we can collaborate with so-and-so must answer not only the traditional question but also an immediately practical one: can we honestly, soberly and practically claim that we are celebrating God's worth and promoting the worth of men and women when we insist on this point?

This last point is a very practical one and we shall have to remember it, not least in the Church of England, as we go through some of the controversial questions which will come up over the next few years. I am not saying that I know which side will prove to be right; I don't. I think that that is what we should be arguing about. We should be asking not only 'Is this Catholic?' in the historic sense but also 'Is it concerned with worth?' in the present sense. For it is quite clear that God is absolutely as much in the present as he was in the past. God has not signed off. We may sign off from him, but I am absolutely certain that he is as livingly present now as he has ever been. The pressure of his presence now is to be perceived through the questions of worth, and everything has to be worked out by mutual accountability.

Thirdly, we have to live in dependence upon, and in openness to, the Holy Spirit. The really important thing about the Holy Spirit seems to be what I have come to call his openness. As he is the Spirit of God, sharing and building up God's worth, he (or she) must be a Spirit which promotes being open to more and more chances of worth, more and more possibilities of service. People who make claims about what the Holy Spirit has told them, when those claims shut them in, must be wrong. For that does not fit with the rest of the picture of God in Jesus who died for all and the Father who is the Father of all. Sometimes people claim the Holy Spirit for what one might call 'little huddles' which keep people cosy in themselves but shut them away from things, and very often special claims about the Holy Spirit split people up. But it seems to me that the Holy Spirit must be a Spirit of openness which (or who) is concerned to make things more personal, make things belong more to persons, help people to understand that the Holy Spirit is God in us. The Holy Spirit is also God between us, giving us the support of one another so that we can face questions that we could not face on our own, and therefore help us to get the strength to look at some things we do not want to look at. All this, all the time, should make our faith more personal: both in the sense of making it deeper and more part of our personality, and in the sense of making us more concerned with persons. In this way the work of the Spirit not only personalizes but universalizes. Anything which God gives us as a very particular or special gift is given us for some outward-going purpose. The church exists for the purposes of God in the world. From the way people talk, it might sometimes seem that the church exists in order to give them their private religious comfort. But that is not true. If you are brought closer to God you will be comforted, but you may be comforted in a way which gives you hell. As my small son said to me long ago: he did not think he would become a friend of Jesus because look what happened to them!

The Holy Spirit is given to give us an intense personal faith, but it must be a personal faith which pushes us outwards and universalizes. At the same time it also particularizes. That is to say, the Holy Spirit is given to us to bring this personal faith, this possibility of worth, this sharing, right down to earth where we are now. If you particularize, you have to choose; and when you choose you may choose differently from other people. That is why there is always a strong risk in serving God in a down-to-earth way. You may choose in a way which other people think differently about or you may choose in a way which gets things wrong. From time to time we all get things wrong.

So there is a tension between personalizing faith so that it goes deeper about persons, and universalizing it so that it is always taking in more and more while at the same time particularizing. That means that the Holy Spirit, among other things, is *the spirit of risk*, precisely because he/she is concerned with the worth of God. God has risked creation, and it has taken the cross to pick it up again. If we are following such a God then we must be taken up into these risks. And in doing so, in responding to the Spirit, the church – any church – must be concerned with certain things.

First, worship. Worship must come at the beginning because worth – worship – is celebrating, contemplating and waiting on the worth and the glory of God. Unless we are centred on the worth and the glory of God, everything else will either fly apart or become dull.

Then, because worship is celebration, contemplation, waiting on the worth and the glory of God, it must be responded to in discipleship: letting God's worth penetrate us by the Spirit so that we grow and are transformed. Following God in the Spirit in the church must mean that all the time we are growing. There must be more. The final growth that we have is to have everything stripped away and die so that we are really dependent on God and everyone else; then we may grow on and on endlessly.

Discipleship is growth, letting God's worth penetrate us by the Spirit. If it is God's worth which is penetrating us, then of course it flows into service, which is sharing God's worth in promoting and serving the worth of our neighbour. Service is not going and badgering your neighbours until they are so agitated and frightened that they come to church.

If we are engaged in service and fight against sin, we may find ourselves involved in something which Christians, apparently, are not supposed to do, which is to protest. For if we are part of the worth of God, then we are to fight against unworthiness and that which destroys worth.

Furthermore, it seems to me that if we are concerned with worship in discipleship, in service and when we are led to protest, then from time to time we may be given prophecy. True prophecy, however, is always a gift from God to people who are being faithful, or are caught up in the way, and people are never entitled to set themselves up as prophets. However, God does sometimes give something to faithful servants to say about applications of his worth and his wrath. For if people are really worthwhile, and a society is getting more and more dedicated to a form of simple, selfish, individualistic consumerism, which really means that as long as you get on, you will be doing the best you can for yourself and society, then there is something to be very angry about. The Old Testament would make it very clear that the wrath of God is liable to fall on such a society.

So we may find ourselves in the position of having to testify to the wrath of God against this or that, and at the heart of this there is conversion and evangelism. It lies at the heart because we all need to be changed into the worthwhileness of God, and everyone should be given a chance of belonging to the community of the worth of God.

Worship, discipleship, service, protest, sometimes prophecy, conversion and evangelism. Those are what the church is for; and in being for those things it will be on earth in order to promote and share and celebrate the worth of God.

PART THREE

Christmas and Easter Sermons

8

Christmas

1984

Christmas confronts us with a baby as the glory of God. The real wonder did not, and does not, lie with angels and shepherds or a guiding star from the East. All these are derived wonders, point-ing to the true wonder, symbolizing the faith and reflecting the glory. The real glory, the lasting glory and the undeniable glory is the baby, who grew up as Jesus of Nazareth to be 'crucified, dead and buried'. But this was the beginning rather than the end: for the God, whom he named with particular intimacy as his Father and whom he served with particular passion, raised Jesus up. So Jesus was known to be Christ the Lord, the power of God's kingdom, the means of God's judgment and the promise of God's future. Thus when we celebrate the birth of Jesus Christ we are confronted with a baby as the glory of God.

This is a simple fact the simplicity of which is so profound that it transforms the world. In the first place it sets a concrete and down-to-earth seal of flesh and blood on the idea of men and women as being in the image of God. Such is the pattern and possibility of the personal life of each one of us that God can take on that pattern and possibility and personality. 'Veiled in flesh the Godhead see, hail the incarnate deity', as Wesley so splendidly puts it. But the 'incarnate deity' is the baby Jesus, the baby who is the centre and focus of so much longing and love and tenderness.

Thus the birth which transforms all births is also an ordinary birth. God shares our human life that in our human lives we may know and grow in the sharing of God and develop in the image of God.

Christmas, therefore, is a time of great wonder and comfort – a magnificent affirmation of our humanity under God and in God. But it is also a time of confrontation. How is this promise and possibility of every birth to be related to the actualities of all births, many of them in so much hunger or lack of love or without the means of development? This confrontation we must live with as we go into 1985. Our living faith and our practical faith will be bound to be both disturbed and disturbing. But here and now at Christmas we may simply and faithfully and thankfully be glad. God has become one of us and by his birth endorsed the promise of every birth. Since the baby Jesus is also the crucified and risen Jesus Christ we may dare to hope that the power and the presence of God is at work to redeem and fulfil that promise that is in every birth. So we celebrate this strong and heavenly affirmation of the possibilities of our lives started here on earth. *This* baby confronts us with the glory of God, so the glory of God is to be glimpsed in every baby and hoped for all babies.

Then, secondly, this simple fact of the baby as the glory of God transforms not only our understanding of ourselves but also our understanding of the whole universe. The genes which produce babies, with the particular and individual characteristics and possibilities of each one, are after all simply complicated chemicals which carry and impart codes. The more we experiment and study, the more we find out about these genetic codes and the chemical and physical transactions which produce them. The more we crack the codes and refine our techniques for discovering the basic physics and chemistry, the more we become clear that the whole of the universe of universes in which we are infinitesimal specks is homogeneous – a vast reality built up into unbelievable complexities and possibilities from certain basic physical energies and interactions. Are we then reduced to nothing in the vastness of the impersonal and indifferent energies and atoms of this universe? Quite the contrary.

We celebrate a baby as the glory of God. We know, therefore, that the physical energies, the chemical transactions and the genetic codes which have emerged within the universe are able to build up not only into the fragile and threatened glory of a human person but also into the receptacle, the vehicle, the embodiment, of the transcendent and eternal glory of God. Every unit of energy in the whole universe is permeated by the possibility of a personal purpose which comes alive in love and is to be fulfilled by love. No wonder therefore that an inspired writer, meditating on the meaning of the birth of the child who became both Lord and Christ, could write: 'and suddenly there was with the angel a multitude of the heavenly host praising God and saying "Glory to God in the highest and on earth peace among men with whom he is well pleased"' (Luke 2.14).

All is to be filled by the glory of God, for all proceeds from the Glory of God who is love; and we, specks in the universe but persons in the image of God, have been called to know this glory, receive this glory and serve this glory. This is the message and the reality and the promise of the baby who is the glory of God. The particularity of this birth shows that we are given the opportunity and the calling to be our particular selves in relation to one another and to God so that we can be part of a universal glory which embraces and fulfils all time, all space and all eternity.

Christmas is not a time to huddle away from the realities of the day-to-day world. It is a time to affirm and celebrate the underlying glory of the whole world and the eternally promised glory of that world in and through the God who has become one of us, to be one with us and at one for us.

This is 'the light that shines in the darkness and the darkness has not overcome it' (John 1.5). Nor will the darkness ever overcome it, for the light is the glory of God and at Christmas we celebrate a baby as the glory of God. Nothing but love could be so totally glorious and so utterly committed, at risk and vulnerable. This one baby speaks as powerfully of the glory which creates, redeems and fulfils everything as all the heavenly splendour and all the choirs of men and angels, and all that we know or shall ever find out about this vast and complex universe. Surely God is with us – both as he needs to be as the lord and glory of all and as we need him to be: God over all but God as one of us; God on the way to be crucified for us; the inextinguishable source of glory.

To wish one another a happy Christmas is not, therefore, an attempt to whistle cheerfully in the dark, it is to speak with conviction and hope of the mystery of creation and birth, of the mystery of ourselves, and of the mystery of love who is at once both God beyond all and the baby with all.

1985

Christmas, as we now observe it in this country, is a very odd mixture. This mixture starts from a date fixed in the fourth century, takes many of its outward forms from customs introduced into England during the nineteenth century by Queen Victoria's Prince Consort and has a heavy top-dressing of late-twentieth-century commercialism.

The date of 25 December for celebrating the birth of Christ first appears at Rome in AD 336. One hundred or so years earlier Clement of Alexandria had suggested 20 May for the possible birthday of Christ. An article in *The Times* last Monday reported new arguments for a date between 24 August and 2 September 12 BC. In either case winter would, of course, be out as far as carols go! But the motive for choosing 25 December to celebrate the birth of Christ at Rome in the fourth century was to set up a Christian feast to replace the pagan winter festival which celebrated the birth of the Unconquered Sun and took place in association with the winter solstice. A midwinter celebration of Christians is therefore nothing to do with the actual birthday of Jesus. That personal detail, like all personal details about Jesus, is totally obscure.

So the date of 25 December has nothing to do with the details of the personal history of Jesus and everything to do with Christian faith confronting the pagans. Life, true life, indestructible life did not depend ultimately on the Sun, that is to say on the god Sol, who was reborn each year after the weakness of the winter, but on the God and Father of Our Lord Jesus Christ, the Jesus Christ who was born in Bethlehem, crucified in Jerusalem and raised up never to die again and to defeat sin and death for us all. Thus Christmas, celebrated on 25 December, has from the beginning been a festival of confrontation between the pagan view of life and the Christian view of life. Christmas, as a Christian festival, celebrates a faith focussed into God through Jesus, in opposition to a secular and pagan acceptance of the mere forces of nature and a secular and pagan indulgence in mere merrymaking as either an anaesthetic or a stimulant in the dark days of winter.

What then of our Christmas celebrations now, faced as we are with so many contributions to a human winter of discontent, when we look, for example, to South Africa or to Northern Ireland or to the Middle East; or when we see so much hunger and famine; or when we consider the strikes and the strife and the uncertainty in our own country? What of our celebration, moreover, when we are threatened by the possibility of a nuclear winter which could blot out all life on our earth? Such things pressing upon us and confronting us daily in our newspapers and from our TV screens make it very clear that we Christians are called to be very faithful and very urgent in putting foward and insisting on the Christian face of Christmas. This we must do against the pagan, secular and commercial mask which is more and more obscuring and distorting the basic, encouraging and shattering message of Emmanuel, *God* with us.

However, we clearly cannot face the challenge of a secularism which simply assumes that there is no God and the challenge of a paganism which turns consumption, success in the personal achievement of wealth and technological manipulation into idols, unless and until we are more and more caught up in the wonder and the reality of God with us, of the incarnation, of the mystery and force of the birth of God as one of us. Let us therefore consider this further so that today we may celebrate, and tomorrow and into 1986 we may face the challenge and enjoy the faith to which we are called.

The beginning of the life of Jesus here on earth would never have been remembered, commented on or made the subject of moving and evocative stories had it not been for the end of that life, an end which turned out to have no end. The man Jesus exercised a ministry to which he believed he was called on behalf of God, his Father, and in relation to the coming of the kingdom of this God. His ministry, in its total conviction and commitment, brought him to rejection, isolation, desolation and death. He died as forsaken by God. But it was not so. The Father in whom he trusted, even to desolation and death, raised him up. This was known to his disciples and so Christianity came into being: initiated, sustained and renewed again and again by the Spirit.

Under the guidance of this Spirit, through the compulsion of their faith and because of the experience of that faith lived out in daily obedience and regular worship, the disciples and fathers of the Christian church became convinced of a decisive newness about God. God had not only done a new and decisive thing in Jesus Christ. He had also demonstrated and declared something new and decisive about himself. This was that his power, his presence, his holiness and his love – in short his very 'Godness' – was not only to be found and encountered hidden in the mystery of his infinite greatness, transcendence and otherness. This very 'Godness' of power, presence, holiness and love was equally to be found and encountered in the flesh-and-blood down-to-earthness and the committed and suffering being-one-of-us of Jesus Christ. Here was God with us, here was God for us. The mystery of God – in all his power and all his love – is present and hidden in the flesh and blood of Jesus, with equal force and equal reality to the way in which the mystery of God in all his power and all his love is present and hidden in transcendent glory and unimaginable holiness. This is the 'great and mighty wonder' which the Spirit begins to reveal to us, of which our faith begins to give us glimpses, and which it will take eternity to learn about and enjoy with fullness.

Now if this is what God has shown to us and been for us in Jesus Christ, then surely the birth of this Jesus is greatly to be celebrated. But it is to be celebrated for the wonder of what God is in Jesus and the wonder of what God does in Jesus. It is not to be celebrated because of any wonders – real, imagined or symbolic – which were, or have become, associated with that birth. Properly used and received, they are witnesses and pointers to the wonder but they do not constitute it. The wonder is, and is constituted by, God being a man, and this involves his being born as a baby.

In the stories which have collected round this birth in the Gospels of Matthew and Luke there is one feature which is particularly relevant to our battle against the paganizing and secularizing of Christmas. This is that the principal characters in the principal stories display obedient trust in God. So it is with Mary in the account in Luke and so it is with Joseph in the account in Matthew. The miracle of God's becoming man is responded to – dare we even say in some sense made possible – by the simple and obedient response of devout and faithful members of God's chosen people. Whatever the details of this supreme miracle, the context is thoroughly human: human beings at their best in response and obedience to God. Into that obedience and response God poured himself and out of that obedience and response God drew his own presence among us.

Thus it is made clearer than ever that Christmas is a particularly focussed celebration of the initiative of God. Here we celebrate the loving down-to-earthness of God which makes possible our collaboration with him in responses of faith, devotion, commitment and obedience. Since there is this intimate connection between God and us, established by him and maintained by him as a continuing possibility, it must be clear to us that no winter of human discontents, not even a nuclear winter, can quench the flame of God's love or freeze out the persistence of God's purpose. How this will be we cannot clearly see, and sometimes our hearts must nearly fail us for fear of the things which are coming upon the earth. But we can resolutely see beyond all those forms of celebrating Christmas which are imported from paganism, grafted on by commercialism and misused even by Christians. Then we begin to see into the heart of the mystery and the reality of God with us and then we know that even our struggles over how we should celebrate Christmas are part of the struggle of the love of God to be with us and to redeem us.

And when we know that, we simply celebrate a great and mighty wonder, a down-to-earth wonder, an intimate wonder, a wonder which is to be celebrated by all the presents we can share, all the music we can sing and all the words we can muster – and then is best contemplated in silence.

1986

Christmas is a claim about creation. To celebrate the Mass of the Christ child with living faith and within the fellowship of the church is to take part in a hymn of praise which makes a statement about the whole universe and about every single and particular thing and person within it. This is made quite clear to us by our two readings from the Bible, if we listen to them clearly, keenly and soberly so that they penetrate our minds and our spirits, rather than letting them simply flow over us with the grandeur of their familiar but barely heeded language.

First, the beginning of the letter to the Hebrews: 'God, who at sundry times and in divers manners spake in time past unto the fathers by the prophets, hath in these last days spoken unto us by his Son, whom he hath appointed heir of all things, by whom also he made the worlds.' The future of all things lies in God's Son, for he is 'the heir of all things'. The very basis and existence of all things also lies in God's Son – 'by whom also he made the worlds'. The claim is total and all-embracing, and reinforced by the way in which the passage goes on: 'who being the brightness of his glory, and the express image of his person, and upholding all things by the word of his power, when he had by himself purged our sins, sat down on the right hand of the majesty on high'. That is to say that the life and activity of the Son in his human existence was the expression of God's very glory and reality and that this is the reality and glory which is even now – and for ever – the expression and activity of God's majesty and rule.

This amazing statement of praise and faith is exactly paralleled in the opening of the Gospel of John. 'In the beginning was the Word and the Word was with God, and the Word was God.' This is, of course, a clear echo of Genesis 1, which starts: 'In the beginning God created the heaven and the earth', and then describes each particular day of creation by the refrain 'and God said . . .' It is

God's word which creates everything: 'And God said "Let there be light, and there was light"' (Gen. 1.3). So, as the opening of John continues: 'The same was in the beginning with God. All things were made by him; and without him was not anything made that was made. In him was life, and the life was the light of men.' Our passages, therefore, make it quite clear that when we are celebrating the birth of Jesus, who came to be known as the Christ of God and came to be worshipped as the Son of God, we are joining in a hymn of praise which joyfully claims that the whole universe is based in, arises from, and will be summed up by, that light and life and love of God which God invested and expressed in the human life of Jesus.

The celebration and the claim are magnificent. And in the right place, like Durham Cathedral, and with the right music, like Christmas carols and Christmas choral music splendidly performed, we can almost persuade ourselves, at least for a moment or two, that we more than half believe it. But it will not stand up to much investigation, will it? Consider what we now know about the universe. It is altogether too vast, too complex and too alien to be thus personalized and encountered as the expression and searching and moving forward of love. It is a bit of a mystery that small specks like human beings should be able to dream such dreams and create such poems and, as Humpty Dumpty might have said, there *is* glory for you, of a sort. But really and truly, and in the end (which for each of us individually must be somewhere between a mere ten or twenty years and a mere seventy or eighty off – and for the whole human race cannot be so far off, even if we do not speed it up with the odd nuclear explosion) – in the end, it cannot possibly be true that we and the universe are one in the possibilities of personal and divine light and life and love. On a clear winter night look at the stars – and reflect – and be put in your place. And then go back to what dreaming and living remains open to us, as long as they do. But do not let us kid ourselves that the Christmas story is more than a superb and moving and comparatively sustained piece of human whistling in the dark. It just claims too much.

Or does it? There is, it seems to me, just one possible way

forward for the faith which joins in and commits itself to the Christmas hymn of praise. But this way forward is only open to us if we are prepared to live with the well-nigh incredible magnitude of what the Christmas faith is claiming and what the Christmas hymn of praise is celebrating. The way forward is this. Supposing it is true that men and women have emerged where they have in the universe (that is, on what we call the earth), and as they are (that is as what we call persons) as 'in the image of God'. This would be to claim that in their exceedingly micro- and diminutive way, men and women in the mystery of their personal being and potentialities are in some basic way programmed on the same wavelength as God. This could only be the case by a remarkable and imaginative act of love and risk on the part of a God, who, if he exists, and if he is the true God of the real universe, must indeed be a mystery who goes amazingly and dauntingly beyond our comprehension. But we might get a hint about our being in the image of God, that is, of our having the derived capacity to resonate – however weakly – on the same wavelength as God, if we carefully consider the amazing human capacity to understand, explore and even to some extent to manipulate the dimensions, powers and possibilities of this universe. Even our discovery of the dimensions which diminish us practically to nothing raises some sort of question about what this near-nonentity is which becomes aware of that which comes near to crushing it into a micro-space of temporary near-nothingness. Might this hint of being in the image of God join up with the magnificence of the Christmas hymn of praise and reinvigorate the possibility of faith, that we are in the image of God and God has chosen to be one of us?

But it won't really do, will it? Look at the way people behave. Look, alas, at the way churches behave and Christians behave. Religion produces quite as much unpleasantness as glory, and so much of the practice of religion is clearly for the benefit of the practitioners, who even want to keep God for themselves and get very worried if God gets portrayed as being too forgiving or if some types of believers get too exploratory or questioning. The human and functional purpose of religion is clearly to shield people from reality and produce an induced warmness which protects them from the cold of actual reality. And in actual reality – that bit of it which we call history, or even current affairs – there is far too much muddle and mess and misery and deliberate waste, cruelty and wickedness to allow us to believe that everything in the vast span of the natural universe and the confused ups and downs of our little earth is somehow or other the expression of, and the material for, the glory of God as he seeks to share the mystery of his holiness, righteousness and steadfast love. The Christian hymn of praise is a particularly moving and gallant example, at least among those who have become culturally aware of it and used to it, of the wistful and agonizing capacity of human beings to dream dreams which seem to reach far beyond them. But it is and remains a dream. It can no more be realistically brought down to earth and cashed than can the credit-card debts incurred by many of those who have been determined to have a good Christmas be paid off in 1987. We just have different ways of deceiving ourselves and making our lives temporarily bearable, or even briefly enjoyable – at least at a consumer level.

Well – I hope you have, in your various ways, faced up to and weighed these things. For otherwise you have probably not prepared for a *Christian* celebration of Christmas. Without some such consideration as I am sharing with you, we shall all just be joining in the current cultural celebration of Christmas, which is a mix between private religious celebration for some and private secular celebration for practically all. But a Christian celebration of Christmas is not to be so domesticated; that is, either shut up in homes or taken as being at home in any culture or society. It confronts us with a cosmic and universal claim and invites us to join in acts of faith and of praise in a God who is a mystery going beyond our imaginations and yet who includes in this mystery a capacity both to reflect himself in us and to be one of us. This, so the hymn of praise says, is because he is really God and he is really love. This is no easy thing to believe. It is neither easy to come to grips with what it really means nor is it easy to hang on to the truth and the reality of the meaning when and if one glimpses it. It

97

is truly a mystery but, so the Christmas hymn of the church insists, truly a possibility.

In his introduction to his Gospel, the author of John makes it clear that he knows how difficult it is to receive what we may well call 'the Christmas message'. 'In him was life, and the life was the light of men. And the light shineth in darkness, and the darkness comprehended it not ... That was the true light, which lighteth every man that cometh into the world. He was in the world, and the world was made by him, and the world knew him not. He came unto his own, and his own received him not.' Picking up the signs of the Creator God is not an easy or to-be-taken-for-granted matter. Likewise it is no easy or to-be-taken-for-granted matter that religious people will get on to what the incarnate God is up to or down to. ('He came unto his own and his own received him not.') Christmas is quite as much a challenge as a comfort, or only a real and lasting comfort in so far as it is received as a challenge.

But the Fourth Evangelist includes in his introduction a word of both great realism and great hope – 'and the light shineth in darkness and the darkness comprehended it not'. The Greek for 'comprehended' is a word (*katelaben*) which sometimes means 'grasp' = 'understand' and sometimes means 'grasp' = something like 'get a hold of and suppress'. Perhaps an English equivalent would be 'master'; that is to say, the darkness could not master the light of Christmas. All the things which give us reason to hold that the Christian message is too much and goes too far in the miseries and the ignorances of the world appear to master it and overcome it, but the darkness cannot do this. Neither the message nor the faith nor the hymn of praise is silenced. Nonetheless it remains the case that the darknesses of this world, including those in our hearts and in our so-called Christian practices, never seem to master the message of light and glory in the sense of 'come to terms with and live up to' the glory and greatness of a God of the whole universe who is also in touch with us and one with us.

So the struggle of light with darkness remains. The mystery and glory of Christmas go with the incredibility and betrayal of Christmas. A proper Christian celebration of Christmas is, therefore, to join in the church's hymn of praise, of faith and of hope and to make this joining in an occasion of renewed resolve, determination and commitment. The commitment must be to a persistent worship and a persevering neighbourliness.

Worship must be persisted in, for it is only by attention to the mystery and glory of God that we can possibly begin to enter into the stupendous implications and applications of the message of Christmas. Neighbourliness must be persevered in because the mystery and the message is about love of cosmic dimensions and particular applications and encounters. So it is in the steadfast and realistic practice of loving our neighbours that we find the opportunities and the fruits of sharing in the love of God. This is the love which is the basis and the promise of the universe, the love which can express both its cosmic reality and its invincible realism in the sign and person of one human being, Jesus of Nazareth who is Jesus Christ our Lord. Amen.

1987

'God, who at sundry times and in diverse manners spake in time past unto the fathers by the prophets, hath in these last days spoken unto us by his Son.' This beginning of the traditional Epistle for Christmas Day reminds us that we cannot rightly and practically begin to understand what Christmas is about unless we pay attention to the way in which the birth of Jesus is seen by the early Christians as the fulfilment of prophecy. Indeed, we Christians who are, surely, deeply concerned about the *religious*, or better, *godly* message of Christmas need very urgently to recapture this prophetic dimension of the Christmas stories. Unless and until we do this we shall be failing to bear witness to what the stories collected around the birth of Jesus in the Gospels of Matthew and Luke have to say about the power, the presence and the promise of God. We shall be leaving these almost too traditional and too often repeated stories to become more and more fairy-tale-like accompaniments to a Christmas that scarcely speaks of Christ. The most the stories will do will be to lend an optional religious tone to activities which are wholly centred on celebratory consumption accompanied by largely unfocussed aspirations of good will. The sharpness, excitement and provocation of the biblical narratives are already largely lost, even among us Christians, and so celebrations of Christmas are in the gravest danger of saying nothing effective or authentic of God.

By referring to 'the prophetic dimension' of the stories told around the birth of Jesus I am drawing attention to the way in which all the stories are steeped in references to, and echoes of, the Old Testament. The stories have much greater depth and many more overtones and undertones than our stylized nativity plays, our Christmas cards and even our Christmas carols readily allow us to perceive. Further, the stories we focus on of shepherds and angels, of the crib and of the 'three kings' (although there is nothing in Matthew about the Magi being kings or even about there being three of them) are isolated by us from their total context in the first two chapters of the Gospels of Matthew and Luke. They become stories detached from the role they play as prologues to the much more important and much more clearly historical business of the life, words, deeds and passion of Jesus of Nazareth.

As an example and indication of the point I am trying to make, let us consider the fact that Matthew introduces what are to us the much more famous and familiar stories about Joseph, about the visit of the Magi and about Herod, the flight into Egypt and the slaughter of the Innocents with a 'genealogy of Jesus Christ, Son of David, Son of Abraham'. As this is his introduction it presumably indicates what he believes himself to be writing about. The genealogy starts with Abraham 'the father of Isaac' and lists father by father until we get to 'Jacob the father of Joseph, husband of Mary, of whom was born Jesus, who is called Christ'. This is clearly a stylized list, arranged in three fourteens, as Matthew himself points out in Matthew 1.17: 'Thus there are fourteen generations in all from Abraham to David, fourteen from David to the exile to Babylon, and fourteen from the exile to Christ.' This is to say that the birth and life of Jesus is to be understood within the total context of God's dealings with Israel and as either the consummation of these dealings or the next decisive stage in them. Abraham was called to be the father of many nations; David was *the* typical king of Israel; and the exile to Babylon marked God's judgment on his people which, because they were indeed his people and he was indeed God, God was bound to redeem and reverse.

Thus the scene is set and the claim is made. It is a claim that what happens in, around and as Jesus is significant of and decisive for all the purposes and promises of God in his total dealings with Israel. It is a claim which emerges from the history of Israel, is significant for all subsequent history and is focussed on the life and history of Jesus from birth to death – and beyond. But it does not follow that the genealogy is itself actual or detailed history.

Indeed, in his genealogy which he puts in at a slightly later stage in his Gospel after the birth stories, Luke has twenty-two names from the exile to Joseph where Matthew has fourteen and he takes his genealogy back to 'Adam the Son of God'. This makes it quite clear that the passages and stories we are dealing with and which we draw on for our familiar Christmas stories are not put forward as descriptive or narrative history but as arguments or claims about what God has been discovered to be doing in and through the life, death and resurrection of Jesus of Nazareth.

Thus Luke, through his genealogy, is making the point that Jesus is central to God's purposes in creation. In this Luke is making exactly the same point as John in his famous prologue which is the traditional Gospel for Christmas day and which we have just heard. The significance of Jesus is tied up with the very Word which is part of God's original and continuing creative activity.

The reason for making these apparently pedantic and possibly tediously critical points on what is supposed to be a high day, a holy day and a holiday is this. If we stick to the Christmas stories on their own, and especially in the way we tend to tell them and use them these days, we not only miss the biblical points of the stories but we probably also betray them. Consider, for example, the tendency to talk about Christmas as 'the season of good will'. This is an echo of part of the message of the angels to the shepherds in Luke 2.14 which in the Authorized Version of the Bible is translated: 'Glory to God in the highest and on earth peace, good will towards men'. It is, however, very generally agreed that this is not an accurate translation of Luke's Greek. What the angels are made to say is something more like: 'Glory to God in the highest, and peace to men on whom his favour rests.' And who are the men on whom God's favour rests? As the rest of the Lukan birth stories makes abundantly clear, these are the men and women who in humble faith and poor circumstances long for 'the consolation of Israel' (Luke 2.25). That is to say they were good and righteous faithful believers who were looking for God to establish his messianic age of holiness, justice and peace.

The point therefore is not the good will of men and women, but that behaviour, intention and purpose of men and women which will be in accordance with God's good will and pleasure. Christmas expressions of good will, such as charitable efforts to remember the poor and the old, or to feed the homeless over Christmas while social security institutions are closed are, of course, all very well in their way, and certainly to be commended and continued. But if we are to respond to the prophetic thrust of the actual narratives and passages such as the Benedictus and the Magnificat in the birth stories of Matthew and Luke, we are required to face up both to God's demands for righteousness and justice, to be sought all through the year, and to God's offer, in and through Jesus Christ who is 'Emmanuel', God with us, always to reinforce, renew and develop such conduct, such longing and such seeking. The message of the birth stories of Jesus is not a Christmas message: it is a universal message about God and about all men and women to be responded to, sought after and developed throughout the year.

A Christian and biblical celebration of Christmas would be a celebration of God's judgment upon all in our society, our world and our families which contradicts his desire for holiness, righteousness and peace, a celebration of God's promise that he is always with those who seek holiness, righteousness and peace in their family, social, national and international lives and a renewal of practical hope in all those things which throughout the year will be moving towards a society where special efforts of good will and charity at Christmas are simply unnecessary. This will be because society, welfare activity, neighbourliness and family life are dealing with the present gross neglect of people and the present gross abuse of the resources of the world which leave homelessness, hunger and loneliness as prominent parts of our affluent and organizationally capable world.

The world and humanity needs much more than occasional outbursts of good will, vaguely focussed and not sustained by systematic grace or persevering hope. And the world and humanity are offered much more. They, we, are offered a God who is with us in promoting peace, justice and holy love, both in people and in the world. We are confronted by a God who condemns our abuses and judges our refusals of neighbourly responsibility and our refusal of sustained uses of our powers to share and to build. Instead we tend to consume and destroy. So, for example, Bethlehem may have been the birth place of the Saviour of the world but now it is a frightened and harrassed place where Muslims and Jews fight and Christians are marginalized or confused. Unless we relearn and rediscover what the birth stories of Jesus are really about we shall just be adding to religious factions and fantasies which offer some of us occasional comfort by escaping from the real world and the real challenge of men and women's bad or weak will in relation to God's glory and good will.

If, however, we can get back to what the birth stories are really about, then we shall be able to hear the angels as they sing both of the glory of God and the possibilities of men and women in whom God is well pleased. We shall also see why those who search the stars for signs of hope and destiny can find in the baby living and lasting signs of the possibility of enduring peace, sufficient justice and real and lasting holiness and worth. But rethinking and renewal of the Christian meaning of Christmas is urgently required of all of us. Since God is God and Jesus is God with us, the strength and the insight to do all this is certainly available to us. So despite our failings, but because of God's promises and presence, Christmas remains for us a time of celebration, an opportunity to enjoy the family and an encouragement to dedicate ourselves to our neighbours and to our whole world in search of God's holiness, righteousness and peace.

9

Easter

1985

Easter is the celebration of the discovery that death could not put
an end to Jesus. We do not just celebrate the survival of Jesus. We
do not even celebrate because God restored the crucified dead and
buried Jesus to life. Easter is not the commemoration of an event
like the raising of Lazarus as portrayed in the Fourth Gospel. Here
a man who had died of sickness and been buried is brought to life
again and restored to his family until he should eventually die. But
Easter is the celebration of the discovery, the claim, the faith and
the assurance that 'Christ, once raised from the dead, is never to
die again; he is no longer under the dominion of death' (Paul, in
Romans 6.9, as translated in the New English Bible).

The resurrection, for our corporate faith and in our personal
faith, is a declaration made by God in Jesus. God declares that he
is the God who raises the dead to life everlasting in his kingdom.
This declaration God makes by raising up this particular man,
Jesus, for 'the truth is, Christ was raised to life – the first fruits of
the harvest of the dead' (Paul again: I Corinthians 15.20). And
'Christ the first fruits' is this historical person Jesus of Nazareth
who preached the kingdom of God, lived for the kingdom of God
and then was put to death for the kingdom of God by the upholders
of religious orthodoxy and the maintainers of governmental law
and order. We celebrate the discovery, and we maintain the faith,

that this Jesus of Nazareth was wholly right. He was right in his total faith in God our Father, he was right in his absolute hope of God's kingdom, and he was right in his unconditional love of, and forgiveness for, men and women, both in their sins and in their neighbourliness. God declared Jesus to be in the right by raising him from the dead and so in Jesus Christ, crucified and raised up, God declared his lordship, his kingdom, his forgiveness of sins and his undefeatable love.

So the resurrection of Jesus Christ blazes forth into the whole world and into eternity. The risen Jesus is preached and believed in as the ascended Christ who is seated at the right hand of God and who will come again to judge the living and the dead at the end of the world and the final summing up of all things into that kingdom of love where 'God will be all in all' (I Corinthians 15.28). The resurrection of Jesus Christ is a declaration of God, through a particular man to a particular series of men and women at a particular period of time of his eternal nature, his persistent purpose and his all-embracing promise. What God has been, and has done, and has declared through and as Jesus, is what God is and what God is doing as he reigns over the universe (for the risen Jesus is 'seated at his right hand') and it is also what God will do in the end and fulfilment of all things (for the risen Jesus will 'come again in glory to judge the quick and the dead', as the picture language of faith symbolizes the hoped-for reality).

Easter, therefore, is the celebration of the initial and the initiating discovery of this declaration of God in Jesus. But to have the authentic and utterly indestructible comfort and joy and glory of Easter, we must dare to believe in the sort of God who has made his declaration in Jesus by the sort of means and through the sort of people he has actually used. All too frequently, I fear, the Easter message, both by those who, up to a point, believe it and by those who reject and ignore it, whether scornfully or wistfully, is read, heard and interpreted in a key or mode which is inappropriate to it. And the misunderstanding lies in a misunderstanding of God. Very often people who believe in God seem to want (and people who cannot or will not believe in God seem to reject) a God of hard and fast guarantees, a manipulating God, an overwhelming

God. But the God who is at the heart of the biblical tradition, the God who is in Jesus and the God who declares himself in the Easter discovery is not like that. This God entrusts himself to men and women in their freedom and in their consequent sin and risks collaboration with them: a collaboration based on his covenant, restored by his sacrifice and renewed by his grace but depending also on human and personal response and faith, discernment and obedience. In such a passionate, artistic and divine work of freedom and love there can be no hard-and-fast guarantees, no manipulation and no overwhelming, save where there is the totally free giving of surrender to overwhelming love which wins the victory, not because it commands or compels, but because it attracts and wholly persuades.

So it is with the resurrection of Jesus Christ from the dead. There is good evidence; it is perfectly reasonable to believe in God's raising of Jesus, and for me it is overwhelming. Just as I am absolutely certain that I shall die, so I am wholly assured that God in Jesus Christ will give me and mine eternal life. Indeed I know I am dying and I know that I am already tasting eternal life. But there is no *proof* of the resurrection of Jesus. Whatever the real and provocative signs by which the first disciples first picked up the reality of God's declaration in the Jesus who had been dead and was now really, personally and for ever alive, they could only evoke a faithful response and start people on a faithful discovery. They could only point to and speak of the resurrection faith. They could neither wholly establish nor wholly prove it. This faith had to grow and establish itself in the power of the Spirit, the fellow-ship of the church, in the living of life and in the facing of death. Likewise with the stories that were eventually told to bear witness to the initial and initiating events and piecemeal discoveries which built up to the steady and never-ending stream of resurrection faith. They are human, they are not always reconcilable, and they can never prove; only provoke and promise and, under God and in fellowship, burst into compelling beams of light and fires of personal assurance.

The Easter discovery was not a stock miracle. It was a growing, and growingly compelling, discovery (shared, as Paul reports in I

Corinthians 15, initially by well over five hundred people, including the apostles and himself) of the newness, the almightiness, the freedom and the down-to-earthness of God. Mary wanted to embrace the recognized Jesus. But she was told not to touch him. Thomas demanded to touch but then did not dare and was told: 'happy are those who never saw me and yet have had faith' (John 20.29). After the walk to Emmaus Jesus was known in the breaking of bread, but as soon as they recognized him he vanished from their sight. The message all the time is 'He is not here, he is risen'. The resurrection is neither to be pinned down nor to be wholly proved. It is to be lived by faith in the God who raised Jesus from the dead and who does and will raise us up with him. For Christ is risen. He is risen indeed. Alleluia.

1986

Let us start our meditation about the reality and meaning of the resurrection of Jesus Christ from a very simple and obvious fact. This is that there is no point in surviving death or permanently avoiding death. This is obvious on simple reflection. What point is there in simply going on and on? But it is underlined by, for example, the terrifying Greek myth of the Sybil of Cumae who was granted her wish for immortality with ruthless literalness by the Greek gods. She was made unable to die but she was not given eternal youth, for she had not asked for it. She was thus condemned to getting endlessly older and older. Nothing could make clearer the inhuman heartlessness of the Olympian gods and the stupidity of wishing to survive. Survival is the last thing we should want.

But while there is no point in survival, there is every point in sharing in the resurrection of Jesus Christ. For the resurrection is *God finding his way to being all in all*. Consider this for a few moments with the help of some passages from Paul. First, here are some extracts from I Corinthians 15.20–28. 'But Christ has indeed been raised from the dead, the firstfruits of those who have fallen asleep' (v.20). 'For he must reign until he has put all enemies under his feet. The last enemy to be destroyed is death. For he "has put everything under his feet" [a quotation from Psalm 8.6].

Now, when it says that "everything" has been put under him, it is clear that this does not include God himself, who put everything under Christ. When he has done this, then the Son himself will be made subject to him who put everything under him, so that God may be all in all' (vv.25–28).

The pattern and the dynamism of Paul's belief here is plain. The resurrection of Jesus Christ from the dead is the first instalment and herald of that final raising of the dead which comes at, and comes as, the end of all things. We may compare what Paul says in the narrative of his appearance before King Agrippa and the Roman governor Festus in Acts 26.22–23. 'I am saying nothing beyond what the prophets and Moses said would happen – that the Christ would suffer and, as the first to rise from the dead, would proclaim light to his own people and to the Gentiles.' The resurrection of Jesus as the Christ is the proclamation, the proof and the promise that God will give 'light to his own people and to the Gentiles'. That is to say, God is establishing a kingdom of light and love which will overcome all that is contrary to the will of God, including death and all forms of sin, destruction and distortion. Consider again (from I Corinthians 15.25): 'For he must reign until he has put all enemies under his feet', and v.28: 'When he has done this, then the Son himself will be made subject to him who put everything under him, *so that God may be all in all.*' As I have already said, the resurrection of Jesus Christ is about God finding his way to being all in all and overcoming everything that stands in the way of this.

All worshippers of God face a grave and very threatening problem. The world which God is supposed to have made is scarcely a godly world and the people who are supposed to believe in God scarcely behave in godly ways. There are glimpses of great glory in the world and achievements of great saintliness among the people of God. By and large, however, the record is not good, and randomness, wrongness and evil seem to have at least as much sway as order, righteousness and goodness. Hence the great longing of all those who are caught up in the possibility of God, in the vision of God, in the presence of God for the time when God will make an end and show that he is God indeed, when God shall become all in all.

The resurrection of Jesus Christ is the beginning, in time and for all time, of that end-time of God. As Paul puts it in Colossians 1.18 onwards, 'He is the beginning and the first born from among the dead, so that in everything he might have the supremacy' (note again the parallel to I Corinthians 15.25, 'For he must reign until he has put all enemies under his feet'). Paul continues: 'For God was pleased to have all his fullness dwell in him and through him to reconcile to himself all things whether things on earth or things in heaven, by making peace through his blood, shed on the cross.' Jesus had set himself to serve God and his kingdom. The powers that be had combined to do away with him. Sin and death had nailed him to the cross. And God had raised him up. This Paul knew, as all the apostles knew, for he had mysteriously but realistic-ally, decisively and conclusively, met the risen Christ. So now already there is the experience, the firstfruits and the beginning of the end time when God shall be all in all.

Consider finally extracts from Colossians 3 (the beginning of which is the traditional epistle for Easter Day). 'Since, then, you have been raised with Christ, set your heart on things above, where Christ is seated at the right hand of God.' Christ is described as being 'at God's right hand' because death is overcome for certain and for ever and because he, Jesus, is now through his Spirit God's right hand of continuing activity for promise and victory. So Paul continues: 'Set your minds on things above not on earthly things. For you died, and your life is now hidden with Christ in God. When Christ, who is your life appears, then you also will appear with him in glory.' The glory of the victory of the end when God shall be all in all has already been declared and displayed in the resurrection, so we begin both to share in it and to look forward to it. Thus this life is already to be practised. In verses 9 and 10 Paul continues: 'Do not lie to each other, since you have taken off your old self with its practices and have put on the new self, which is being renewed in knowledge in the image of its Creator.' The original purpose of creation, that men and women, being in the image of God, should share in the glories of God's creation and of God himself in his love, is being restored and achieved through the resurrection. Therefore, as Paul says in the next verse (v.11): 'Here there is no Greek or Jew, circumcised or uncircumcised, barbarian, Scythian, slave or free, but Christ is all, and in all.' Once more we observe the 'all in all'. Just as sin, destruction and death are being overcome, so are the divisions and alienations of peoples, races and classes. The risen Christ is God's way to the city of God where, because God is all in all, all shall live with all in the fullness of mutual diversity, mutual support and mutual enjoyment.

Therefore it is clear that it is a truly dreadful and diminishing mistake to suppose that the resurrection of Jesus Christ is about either his survival or the survival of you and me. God has not enabled Jesus to survive death; God in Jesus Christ has overcome death and all its allies of randomness, chaos, distortion, destruction and sin. So, God in Jesus Christ does not offer us survival after death but a share in the resurrection from the dead. That is a share in God's victory over all that is contrary to his holiness, his glory and his love and a share in the everlasting excitement, life, joy and peace which is there wherever and whenever God is all in all.

And that is why Paul, with great practicality and down-to-earthness, ends his great resurrection chapter, I Corinthians 15, thus: 'Therefore, my dear brothers, stand firm. Let nothing move you. Always give yourselves fully to the work of the Lord, because you know that your labour in the Lord is not in vain.'

1987

'For as yet they knew not the scripture that he must rise again from the dead' (John 20.9).

This is the last but one verse of the traditional Gospel for Easter Day which we have just read. The last verse of the reading is even more down-beat. 'Then the disciples went away again to their own home.' If *that* is the Gospel for the day, what are we getting excited about? For Easter Day is supposed to be *the* high-point of the Christian year, yet the traditional Gospel for the day presents us with puzzlement over an empty tomb and people going home again.

As I have been using the comparative quiet of Holy Week to read around in the New Testament and meditate about a sermon for Easter Day I found myself thinking: surely, the lectionary could do better than that. Are there no 'Easter spectaculars' which could be read for the Gospel of the day? But then I found a train of thought developing and it is this train of thought which I shall now try to share with you.

This particular Gospel reading faces us with the question 'Why did God empty the tomb?' Or to put it more generally: 'What was God doing when he brought about those events and experiences which convinced some of those men and women who had been with Jesus, and who had seen Jesus die, that this same Jesus was alive "beyond death"?' Clearly God was not just moving a corpse out of a tomb or just making Jesus alive again. This is made clear by the stories of commissioning and empowering which are told of the risen Jesus in the Gospels and by the rapid growth of Christian preaching and of membership in the Christian movement which is reported and reflected in the rest of the New Testament.

You will remember that the Gospels of Matthew, Luke and John all have what we may call commissioning stories connected with the risen Jesus. They are all different: Matthew puts his story in Galilee while the other two put theirs in Jerusalem, but all the stories have the same thrust and point. The last verses in Matthew's Gospel read, in part: 'Then the eleven disciples went to Galilee, to the mountain where Jesus had told them to go. Then Jesus came to them and said, 'All authority in heaven and on earth has been given to me. Therefore go and make disciples of all nations . . .' Luke has the eleven 'and those with them' assembled in Jerusalem when Jesus appears among them, and the incident ends: 'Then he opened their minds so they could understand the scriptures. He told them: "This is what is written; the Christ will suffer and rise from the dead on the third day, and repentance and forgiveness of sins will be preached in his name to all nations, beginning at Jerusalem. You are witnesses of these things. I am going to send you what my Father has promised; but stay in the city until you have been clothed with power from on high."' This is picked up at the beginning of Acts (which is a continuation of the Gospel of Luke) where, as a prelude to his ascension, Jesus says: 'But you will receive power when the Holy Spirit comes on you; and you will be my witness in Jerusalem, and in all Judaea and Samaria, and to the ends of the earth' (Acts 1.8). That promise is, of course, picked up a few days later at Pentecost according to Acts. In chapter 20 of John's Gospel there is likewise an incident in Jerusalem on the evening of the first day of the week when Jesus appears in a locked room and, among other things, says: '"Peace be with you! As the Father has sent me, I am sending you." And with that he breathed on them and said, "Receive the Holy Spirit. If you forgive anyone his sins, they are forgiven; if you do not forgive them, they are not forgiven"' (John 20.21–23).

This appears to be John's equivalent of Pentecost, the giving of the Holy Spirit to the disciples straight away as part of the risen appearance of Jesus, rather than the command to wait for the empowering of Pentecost as in Luke. As I have already said, the stories are all different, and simple inspection of them shows that they cannot be fitted together as a matter of flat narrative sequence. All, however, are, in their own ways, making very much the same point. What God has done and is declaring in raising Jesus from the dead is of significance for the whole world and is to do with overcoming sin. If you ask about the Gospel of Mark, the answer is that it is now generally agreed that the Gospel of Mark itself ends after 16.8, where the women flee from the tomb and tell no one. The last half of chapter 16 is a collection of bits tagged on and reflecting the stories in the other Gospels, so we have no independent commissioning story from Mark. Nonetheless the same point is made: God's raising of Jesus from the dead is of universal significance, and a world-wide mission follows.

Now, what is the scope and dynamic of his universal mission and how is it related to what we have come to call 'the resurrection'? This is where we come back to our text: 'For as yet they knew not the scripture that he must rise again from the dead.' This is one of a number of indications scattered through the stories at the end of the four Gospels which indicate that the events and experiences which convinced Jesus's followers of his resurrection required

113

both time and interpretation to discover what was really going on and what it really meant. This, surely, is what we would expect if we are having to do with something which is both real and really makes a difference to the way in which we ought to approach the whole world. Mere miracles and manipulations must be insufficient. Nothing less than a series of living encounters with the aid of the living God could possibly produce or begin to justify a conviction of cosmic significance – such as is reflected, for example, in Matthew 28.18, 'Then Jesus came to them and said "All authority in Heaven and earth has been given to me"', and in the parallel commissioning and empowering narratives to which I have referred. This is why we cannot begin to approach the matter of the resurrection of Jesus Christ from the dead without bringing in the Spirit and relying on the aid of the Spirit. As Paul says, most clearly in Romans 8, unless the Spirit of the God who raised up Jesus Christ is at work in us and through us, we neither live in nor are capable of sharing with others the faith generated by the risen Christ.

For what was discovered, by a few chosen and intimate followers of Jesus, women who cared for him and Galileans who followed him, even if they betrayed him at crisis point in the Governor's praetorium, was that Jesus's devotion to God his Father and Jesus's commitment to the kingdom of his God and Father was neither an illusion nor a misplaced commitment. It had taken him to the desolation of believing that his God had forsaken him. But this sacrificial obedience, like the obedience of Abraham who was ready to sacrifice his God-given heir in Isaac, had been accepted and vindicated. God had raised him up. So it turned out, and it had painfully but joyfully to be discovered, that all this was 'according to the scriptures'. This is to say that Jesus's way of serving the kingdom and his Father both fitted into those patterns of God's revealing and saving dealings with men and women which had constituted and shaped the experiences and scriptures of Israel and also gave them a decisive turn. God's way of bringing his holy, righteous and loving purposes to the world and of extending them from Israel to all was Jesus.

As we try, with longing and prayer, with praise and hope, to be caught up into this faith, this mission and the reality of this life in the Spirit, we need to note that all this had been discovered in the growing Christian movement and worked out by preaching and service and by the Spirit-inspired reflections and writings of such as Paul well before the Gospels were written down. This, I am sure, is a principal reason why the resurrection stories in the Gospels are so fragmentary, so piecemeal, at times so inconsistent and so fragile as far as persuasion and proof goes for any but those who already believe. They simply reflect and report on a living, vibrant, realistic and powerfully-recruiting faith. They are not the basis of and the sole evidence for that faith.

So there are no 'Easter spectaculars' in the Gospel accounts. These simply reflect, point back to and resonate with the original cumulative, personal and faith-filled discovery by the first Christian women and men that Jesus, his life, his continuity, his hopes and his challenges had not been cancelled by his crucifixion. Instead, God had vindicated him by making it known to some of those who had followed him and cared for him that beyond the cross, beyond the grave and therefore beyond the apparently finalizing power of death, Jesus was alive, as himself, but established by God as a foretaste of the resurrection hope of all.

The personal and spiritual processes involved in this unexpected, amazing, and potentially earth-transforming discovery can be to some extent perceived if we are not trapped into comparing and contrasting details and expecting to produce public proofs. The discovery that Jesus was alive in a new and decisive way because God had raised him up began with puzzlement, fear and uncertainty. Then there accumulated experiences and appearances and opportunities of understanding, contextualizing and exploring which were decisively persuasive about both the reality of the living of Jesus and his undoubted identity with the Jesus of Galilee and the Jesus of the cross. And then the propaganda began. To show how earth-shaking it all was, stories of earthquakes got around and Matthew put them into his version of the stories. People argued whether Jesus was real or a ghost. (Paul and the whole early church knew, of course, that he was real indeed, as real and alive at the Spirit!) Being two generations or so from the original impact and dynamic, stories were made *ben trovato* and we get the excessively bodily and physical stories which turn up in Luke – and, perhaps, in John. These are stories which, almost certainly, Paul would have found unnecessary, or even slightly contradictory. But the point is not that they were made up in modern fashion to deceive. They grew in ancient fashion to witness to what the first disciples knew well enough: Jesus was really alive, Jesus was really the same Jesus as they knew in Galilee and as died upon the cross, and therefore Jesus was Lord 'according to the scriptures'. He was therefore decisive for our understanding of God and of God's plans, patterns and purposes of salvation for the whole world.

The traditional Gospel for the day – with its note of puzzlement, unfinished business and need to work things out 'according to the scriptures' – remains perfectly appropriate because, in the Gospels, there are *no* 'Easter spectaculars'. If you want an Easter spectacular read Romans 8 (earlier, of course, than any Gospel account) where Paul gloriously meditates on how the Spirit of the God who raised up Jesus shows us – as adopted sons and daughters – that we are on the way of sharing in the redemption of the entire cosmos. Or read II Corinthians 3–6, where Paul works out the relation between death and resurrection and the episodes of life in the body, relating it all to God's purposes in creation as reflected in Jesus. Or consider the spectacular growth of the early church, or marvel at the faith and work of Mother Teresa and her friends, or, as we have been recently reminded here in Durham, recall the bravery and hope and humour of Desmond Tutu and his friends.

For the Easter liturgy we have to focus, through the fragmentary and later records of discovery and growth in the resurrection faith, on worship of the God who raised up Jesus, on the reality and promise of the Jesus who is seated at his right hand and on the power of the Spirit who invites us also into resurrection faith, into resurrection life and into resurrection hope.

1988

Today we celebrate all Christian celebrations. For Easter Sunday is the Sunday of all Sundays. This is so because Easter Day is the celebration of that which is celebrated by Christians every Sunday and the celebration of that which made Sunday the first day of the week. As you have doubtless observed, most calendars now put Sunday at the end of the week. Sunday is now part of the 'weekend' – when people have time off – and when that small minority of people who still feel called to practise Christian observance are incidentally free to 'go to church'. Sunday is no longer a compelling and powerful celebration for life as a whole or for society as a whole. But we will come back to that.

What we are celebrating in this celebration of celebrations and on this Sunday of Sundays is that initial compelling discovery of the liveliness of Jesus which persuaded a small but sufficient number of the men and women who had been his followers and friends that Jesus's death on the cross and his burial in a tomb were not the terminal events in his service of God and in his search for the kingdom of God. Jesus was not dead, although he had been put to death. Something quite extraordinary had happened. It was so extraordinary that, initially, there was a good deal of uncertainty, disturbance, confusion and, in some ways, fear.

This is reflected in the stories in the Four Gospels which, in various ways, offer accounts of some of the episodes, incidents or experiences which constituted, lay behind or contributed to the common conviction and faith that the placing of Jesus's dead body in a tomb was not the terminal event in his service of, and search for, God's kingdom. People continue to produce little books which attempt to show that the accounts in the Gospels contained in what we call 'the resurrection stories' are, in fact, satisfactorily reconcilable with one another and that, what is more, they 'prove' the resurrection of Jesus. I believe this to be a faithless, useless and even dangerous exercise.

First, and less importantly, the accounts cannot possibly be honestly and coherently reconciled according to modern criteria of historicity and coherence. It is quite impossible to reconcile, in a journalistic and modern flat and literal way, the young man dressed in a white robe of Mark, together with the fear of the women Mark records, with the earthquake, the angel and 'the

117

women filled with joy' of Matthew (in exact opposition to Mark), or with the 'two men in clothes that gleamed like lightning' of Luke (John, incidentaly, has no messenger or angels at the tomb at all). Myth-making and story-telling built up to make a point is obviously going on. It is an offence to God, who if is he is God can cope with and work through all realities, including the reality of the human tendency to improve a story, to pretend otherwise. It is also an offence to the commonsense and searching for truth of our fellow human beings to try to pull wool over their eyes or to ask them to believe the evidently incredible. Likewise, although I do not have time to go into the details in this brief sermon, it is quite impossible to construct a satisfactorily coherent inter-weaving of the Jerusalem traditions of the appearances and the Galilean ones. What *is* clear is a tension and a dynamic between them, bearing witness to a common conviction, developed in ways of which we cannot now get the details (only some glimpses) that the significance, the life and the personality of Jesus was not terminated by his death and burial.

Secondly, and more importantly, what is supposed to be achieved by these attempts at alleged reconciliation of the details of the story and the consequent claim to 'proof'? Even if the attempts were overwhelmingly conclusive to the most detached outsider (which they evidently are not), is it supposed or claimed that they would thereby convert the said outsider to Christian faith and to whole-hearted membership of the Christian community? Clearly they would not. The happening of an extremely mysterious and unlikely event, even if it is of a man coming alive again after an undoubted death, is just that – the establishing of an extremely mysterious and unlikely event. The question for faith or for hope or for wonder or for praise is still 'so what?' What is going on here? What is this part of? How does this reach out into the whole of human life and the whole of the world we live in?

This point, about the faith which is evoked by the resurrection and the proclamation and possibilities which are enabled by it, is nicely illustrated by the current matter of the postmark which says 'Jesus is alive'. I leave on one side any question about whether or not this is an appropriate use of a public service and a sensitive and humane way of evangelism. I simply point out that if 'Jesus is alive' is meant to reflect the Easter message, it is biblically and theologically inadequate. The Easter message is 'Christ is risen'. This is not a message about the man Jesus. It is a message about what God is doing, what God is proclaiming and what God is offering in, through and around the man 'Jesus of Nazareth'.

After all, if I understand it correctly, the Muslims hold that Jesus is alive. He was, indeed, according to the Koran, a prophet of God – the next most important prophet to Mohammed. As such a prophet he could not be allowed to die and God did not allow it. How God did not allow his death in the circumstances of Gethsemane and the crucifixion is a matter for dispute over the exegesis of certain Koranic texts and a matter of different traditions in subsequent Muslim reflection (one such tradition is the story about Jesus ending up in Kashmir). But, as far as I can see, 'Jesus is alive' is a perfectly acceptable statement to a Muslim. Also, there is at least one Jewish writer who has argued that the resurrection narratives convince him that, as with at least the prophet Elijah, Jesus the prophet was caught up to be with God. Jesus's being alive, therefore, while it is necessary to the resurrection faith and celebration, is not centrally and decisively what the resurrection is about.

The resurrection is about God's vindication of the ministry, message, person and presence of Jesus. His death and burial were not the terminal events in his service of God and his search for the kingdom of God his Father. As it is put, for example, in Acts 2.36, 'God has made this Jesus whom you crucified, both Lord and Christ.' That is why the heart of the celebration of celebrations at Easter is best pointed to by the wondering, joyful and promising cry 'Christ is risen.'

The resurrection was all that God did at the first Easter to enable Jesus's disciples and friends to discover that Jesus was indeed alive and that Jesus, therefore, was the Christ of God. The reality and meaning of Jesus's resurrection cannot be properly understood outside the context of all the events to do with Jesus and the way in which he placed these events in the context of biblical and Jewish expectations, together with the ways in which

119

his disciples picked up and developed this context and this under-standing. The resurrection is not a single event which bears its revelatory and decisive significance stamped on its surface as a mere happening. The resurrection is a decisive episode in the dealings of God with the world in and through Israel, which gives the story and direction of these dealings a distinctive and decisive significance in and through Jesus.

This meant – and this means – that Jesus's way of life, Jesus's whole-hearted and totally sacrificial caring for the kingdom of God and for the human neighbour, Jesus's obedient suffering and Jesus's passion, death and burial were and are actually and really God's way of coping with all in this mysterious, promising and yet distorted and threatening universe which denies, distorts or diminishes God's kingdom. That is to say that Jesus in his flesh and blood, Jesus in his proclamations and promises, and Jesus in his desertions and desolations, is God's way of making plain that he is indeed God, that he indeed has a kingdom and that this kingdom of holiness, justice, peace and steadfast love is at work in this world and will achieve its aims, purposes and end through this world and beyond this world in the fulfilment of this world. Thus the resurrection is not a religious and cultic event about Jesus being alive as the promise of some sort of survival for those who adhere to his cult; it is a cosmic and divine declaration that Christ is risen as a promise and a provocation to all humanity that God's purposes of holiness, justice and love are alive in our world and are not to be defeated.

This is why concentration on attempts to tidy up the witness of the resurrection stories or to claim them as proofs of some sort of single events are not only useless but maybe dangerous. For they tend to concentrate interest on the wrong point, namely whether we may be quite sure, apart from faith and corporate perception, that this happened instead of challenging us to enter in to what all this is about. And 'all this' of course includes Pentecost, the explosion of the churches around the Mediterranean and, through history, out into the whole world; the fellowship, worship and eucharists of the churches; the witnesses, martyrdoms and service of disciples in many times and many places and the continuing outbursts of liveliness which renew, even as they disturb and provoke, the somewhat confused and uncertain churches which we now have in this country.

What we celebrate today, therefore, is the liveliness of God which God embodied in and expressed through Jesus whom God raised from the dead. Therefore we know, on behalf of the whole world and as a gift and service to the whole world, that holiness, justice, peace and love are always and everywhere at work. Neither our sins, nor other people's sins, nor the appalling disasters and non-senses of the world and history, nor despair and death can or will defeat that God of holiness, justice, peace and love who has declared himself in and through Jesus Christ our Lord. So we are free to celebrate indeed. And we are called, through our celebration, to a service which is joyful, hopeful and concerned with the fate and the future of the whole world. Sunday may have been secularized into being at the weekend. But that is simply our context and our challenge calling us so to praise God and so to serve our neighbours that these neighbours may rediscover with us that what Sunday celebrates is a life which cannot give up hope, will not abandon justice and is sure both of the suffering and of the victory of love. For it is the very life of God.

PART FOUR

Applied Spirituality

10

Why Pray?

Some people have thought and felt and found that there is more to people than people and more to the world than the world. That is why they pray. They reach out to 'the More', they reach in for 'the More'. They fear and they fantasize. They trust and they hope. They plead and they grovel. They long for and they find peace. They believe their prayers are answered in magical and manipulatory ways. They find the heart of prayer in waiting attentively on an Absence who becomes a Presence of great promise, whose deep intimacy remains a distant and wonderful mystery. For such people at such moments prayer is not wanting but being.

Praying has thus been around as a human activity for a long time in a vast variety of forms: some attractive, some unattractive and all, from one point of view or another, questionable. What ought we to make of prayer now, furnished as we are with psychological understandings of dependency and projection, sociological understandings of the bonds of ritual and cult, historical understandings of the manipulatory wickedness of religion, and scientific understandings of a universe of immense complexity, all explicable in terms of the evolutionary capacities of its own space-time, and all on a scale which reduces us to infinitesimal specks who happen, for the briefest moment, to be capable of self-consciousness? What we ought to make of prayer under these circumstances of knowledge and understanding depends, I believe, on what prayers makes of us. ('By their fruits ye shall know them', Matthew 7.16

ff.). The only reason for praying is that one must pray, and the only difficulty about praying is that one cannot pray.

Once you get caught up in praying there is nothing to do but go on, however stubborn, threatening, hidden or confusing the way is. But two things seem to be needed to get anyone caught up in this authentic praying which will not let us go because, above all, we want to go wherever the praying will take us. The first is the incidental, or even accidental, encounter which starts us off, or causes us to find out that we have started. The second is getting through and beyond the practices of religion to the first enticing traces of a godliness which is so infinite, so deep and so steadfast that it promises to embrace, absorb, overcome and fulfil all the depths and dependencies of psychology, all the bonds and structures of sociology, all the aborted promises and distorted hopes of religion and all the complexities and dimensions of evolutionary space-time.

Such an engagement with such godliness is clearly both a deep mystery and a tall order. Outside the moods and modes of prayer it may well seem to the disengaged mind or to the indifferent and unaroused spirit to be the product of some psychological mechanism which has effects equivalent to a drug like LSD. Hence the ever present issue of 'by their fruits ye shall know them'. It can never be compilations of prayers, nor rituals of prayer, nor teaching about prayer or of techniques for praying which validate, authenticate or probabilify praying as a central human way of engaging with proffered and promising Reality. This possibility and promise can be sustained only by the life of prayer and by the life of pray-ers, those who pray persistently. The initial invitation to prayer and the initiating involvement with prayer can only be caught at some point through the personal and individual incidental or accidental encounter to which I have already referred. The biblical traditions refer to this feature of engagement with the presence and possibility of the God, who is 'the More' and who is available for engagement, in terms of 'calling'.

This indicates that the praying I am trying to talk about is not something which is, so to speak, genetically built in to the nature of things so that once the appropriate level of human nature and

126

human consciousness is reached then everyone does it, more or less, and more or less naturally. Rather, the possibility of prayer and the response of prayer are opportunities which are around in the mysterious space which exists between God, who is the infinitely worthwhile possibility of all possibilities, and the universe, which exists and develops because God has risked both these possibilities and this space. This is the space into which human self-consciousness can reach out, thereby 'transcending', as it were, the stuff which is the basis for people being people, just as it is the basis of the world being the world. In this possibility of reaching out lies the possibility of encountering, exploring and developing in a free space where the God who is more than all can be encountered as the God who reaches in. Transcendence and in-dwelling can come together in a free communication, conversation and communion of wonder, mystery and love. But this cannot come about by rote or routine or rule-like regularity, for the freedom, the space, and the response and the receiving of grace, would then be gone – or never available – and prayer would not be praying but programming.

Hence there is no way into prayer except through what we must experience and receive as an incident or even an accident. Some encounter or other, or some discovery or other, has to start us praying or enable us to discover that we have already been praying. If there is any authenticity or realistic resonance in the biblical patterns of prayer, experience and practice, then it will be the case that the intimately personal nature of the call to exploratory and expectant prayer will be most often set off by experiences and encounters which go with membership of, or being on the fringe of, or even directly reacting against, one of the communities of those who have developed and cherished a habit of telling stories about encounters with God. These encounters and the stories reflecting them act as the focus of the community's identity and the stimulus and directive to the community's life. God in the stories and patterns and practices of the people who form the focus of the Bible is a God who gets in touch to share and develop his purposes which turn out to be purposes of holiness, justice, peace and steadfast love.

Praying is, as often as not, triggered off by finding oneself caught up in the story, counted in, or on the fringe of, belonging to the people whose calling is to know God and then plunged into following up what we have glimpsed and what has got hold of us. The world may often be a wilderness, but this very wilderness is the location of a pilgrimage, an exploration, a journey and a struggle which partakes of, and builds up to, a shared purpose which is a purpose and community of worth and of love. The response of prayer and the exploration of prayer are not projections of psychological self-deceit nor fantasies induced by drugs or drug-equivalents but a series of realistic and ever-developing paths which lead into an always expanding reality and develop an always increasing capacity for both realism and hope.

But this will be so only if the journey of prayer, the attentiveness of prayer and the waiting of prayer takes one beyond and beneath the practices of religion and the rituals of religion which may well have triggered off one's attempts at, and experiences of, praying. Institutional religion and its various practices and formulations are simply the deposits formed in history, at various stages of history, by organized attempts to respond to, record and pass on those encounters with the God of mystery behind, within and beyond all things which have led people into ways of praying, practising, worshipping and responding which have endured. If the Reality to which prayer and worship are attempting to respond and explore is really there and really living, then no institutions or formulations or practices will be adequate to that Reality.

Prayer must therefore never be constrained by religion. It may well be started by it and from it; it may well, up to a point, be supported and fed by it; but prayer must go beyond religion. Prayer is a growth in free openness to the open freedom of the mysterious, infinite and lovingly worthwhile God. This God is the God of all who is the mystery within all and beyond all. Such a God may work through encounter and call with particular people, but he (or she or it) cannot be confined to such people and their calling cannot be confined to their own purposes and their own future. Praying therefore cannot be in order to develop our particular souls or selves, but must be in order to abandon ourselves

128

to, express ourselves through, and receive ourselves from, a presence, a possibility, a promise and love which is striving in all, through all, for all.

It is vital, therefore, not to mix up praying with being religious. If religion, in any of the forms known to us, has the last word, then prayer is a joke in very bad taste. For all religions seem to speak of a universality of God and a God of universality and yet be concerned in practice with the promoting of the good of their own adherents, both here and hereafter. Religion may speak of free grace, unrestricted worth and invincible and totally ungrudging love, but somehow or other this gets focussed to the exclusive benefit of those who adhere, proclaim and practice. Religious practitioners seem unable to take with absolutely liberating serious-ness the profoundly theological observation of Groucho Marx that he would not want to belong to a country club that was prepared to elect him to membership. God's grace must set us free for prayer. We do not have to pray in order to reach God's grace, and the setting free must be without end or limit or restriction. In fact prayer is the practice of openness, risk and vulnerability to an ever-increasing range of depth, scope and possibility which is made possible because it is supported by the worth, the value and the steadfast love of God.

The basic reason for praying, therefore, is that we have some glimpse, echo, hope or suspicion that somewhere at the heart of things, and therefore available in and through things, is a love that makes for justice, peace and worth. We pick this up because others have also picked it up, and once we have caught a glimpse we find ourselves caught up, and the praying has to go on from there. There are things around which, provided that we have caught some echo or glimpse of the possibility of prayer, may well en-courage us to take the invitation seriously or help us to direct and deepen our prayer.

These include all the glimpses of God, his glory, his purposes and his promises which we may receive from the Bible and from worship, provided that we remain free or are given freedom to let the stories, the patterns, the poems and the prayers speak for themselves. We must not feel constrained to insist or expect that

129

the 'messages' will come across in some especially religious way or within some superimposed and restrictive dogmatic framework. Once our faith is based on, explored through and developed by prayer, then we are free to receive all the help and hints and corrections that are available through religious scriptures, through religious practices and religious traditions. But I must repeat that religion on its own is a great enemy of the prayer of faith that I am seeking to describe and can easily persuade outsiders that prayer is superstition, magic and manipulation. At the same time far too few insiders actually grow in the faith and practice and promise which is liberating into God and under God.

A particular invitation to, and strengthening of, faithful and patient praying is that pattern of Jesus's life, passion and death as it is variously presented in the four Gospels. This Jesus who lives by intimacy with his Father and lives for the kingdom and glory of his Father is crucified by the guardians of religion and of public order. His way of faith and life is, however, vindicated to his disciples by the knowledge which is given to them of his Resurrection and by their subsequent and consequent empowering with the Spirit. For those who are caught up in this story, that is for those who come to share Christian faith, there is a very clear invitation and encouragement to follow a way of prayer which is humbly open to God in and through whatever happens, perseveringly open to the neighbour for the mutual good God offers all, and steadfastly ready to wrestle with evil, disappointment and desolation in obedient hope. In so doing what Paul calls the folly of Christ's cross will resonate with the folly of belief in God and of expectation of love in the universe as we now know it and society as we now experience it. This resonance will both give reality to prayer and receive reality from prayer and then strengthen the faith that prayer is not a running away from, but a facing up to the realities of which we are a part and the opportunities which are offered to us. We pray because in Jesus we pick up the message that the Reality behind all that is is also involved in the details and distresses of those particular things which concern and trouble us.

But does it make any sense to proceed and to pray as if 'the Reality behind it all', when the 'all' is the immense and impersonal universe known to us, is actually open to us, our concerns and collaboration? Clearly this is a critical matter for faith and for prayer. My approach throughout has been to argue that once we are started in praying we go on, on the basis of prayer, to face and live with questions such as this. What is decisive for response, for faith and for praying is what one believes one is encountering and how it is shaping and directing living and exploring and persevering.

But I would suggest that an additional support for prayer is the exciting and provocative fact that the infinitesimal and briefly self-conscious human beings who have emerged as us in our tiny corner of the universe are able to appreciate, map and respond to the immensities, as well as the microscopic complexities, of this universe whose size totally baffles any imagination even though we can numerically calculate and cope with it. I find this lends at least plausibility to the claim that despite our momentariness we are, in some real sense, in the image of the God who is behind, through and in it all. So we are not only free to pray but encouraged to pray, as long as we realize that the mystery with whom we are resonating is infinitely great and never to be trammelled within the confines of our own religious imaginations and articulations. But the contact, the possibility and the openness is nevertheless there to be responded to and collaborated with. So we should 'pray without ceasing'.

In this prayer without ceasing, prayer as a way of life and prayer as the plunging into life, we are offered the opportunity of following up every hint we receive that our existence may have emerged as an accident but can be received as a gift. We have the opportunity of exploring by prayer into that free space where our emergent liveliness interacts with the steadfast liveliness of God. So we can also learn, in prayer, that dependence is freedom and life, not bondage and extinction. We pray, therefore, because we must, because we may, because we can, because we hope and because we love. We pray as individuals who are encountered, called and impelled, and we pray in worship and in community. Prayer is wonder, waiting, longing, wrestling and responding. It is never magic, manipulation nor power for ourselves. Rather it is that set of the practices of silence, attention, sharing and exploring which strips religion bare of external symbols and accidental accumulations and set us free for openness to all that is and for the pursuit of godliness. This is a practice and pursuit, a stripping and an openness which we can dare to enter into because, from the beginning, prayer is a response to an invitation and, all along, prayer is the waiting for a presence and the promise of a communion.

11

Spiritualities for the End of a Century

The pressures we are under and the uncertainties by which we are surrounded force us back on the fundamental question what it is to be a Christian.

Each of us have our version and experience of these pressures, professionally and personally. On a broader front it is clear that Christians are very much in a minority and the Church of England has many of the characteristics of an obsolescent survival, with the bankruptcy of many of its institutions a real possibility. Our society is under terrific pressures politically,and culturally we have a pluralism and fragmentation that we have scarcely begun to live with. What is more, our condition could easily become apocalyptic.

However, in all this we have to go on from and with what we have. And that raises the question: going and trying to go where?

In this way we are led to look again at the resources of the Christian tradition and to ask: What have they been thus far? How do they operate now? How do they enable us to face up to our highly uncertain and possibly quite limited future?

The situation is highly complex; the questions are very simple. Can we spot any simplicities with which we may live in the complexities?

The spotting of relevant simplicities is surely a basic method of procedure for faith. But the simplicities must be such that they enable us to be open to the complex realities. Alleged simplicities which shut us off from these realities are already denying the Christian tradition from which we claim to draw simplicity. We must be very careful to avoid burying ourselves in regressive nostaliga.

For according to the Christian tradition, as it rests on and grows out of the Bible, *God is in reality*.

That is to say that it is God who is the true and ultimate Reality ('I am the Lord ... and my glory I will not give to another', Isaiah 42.8). It is also to say that God works in and through the realities of contemporary history and experience. This is the basic prophetic insight, and in this connection it should be noted that the Bible is not 'biblical'. The power and insight which led to 'canonization' were always contemporary. There is a great need to set the Bible free so that God can speak to us now 'as he did then' – which does not mean in biblical language and forms but in contemporary language and forms which have the same sustaining, guiding and illuminating power now as the 'biblical' forms and language had in their own time.

So if the simplicities we seek are to be validly and traditionally Christian they must be open to any present complexities. If our use of the Christian tradition which has so far nurtured us shuts us off from manifest contemporary realities and insights then we are manifesting practical atheism rather than faithfulness. This is a thing that the church and numerous groups seem to be doing only too often.

Examples are only too readily to be found in attitudes to sexuality which totally ignore psychological insights, and so prevent us witnessing as we should to the contemporary demands and offers of chastity and for the restoration of sexuality as a crucial sphere of human relationship and offering. Much sounding off about law and order does not promote a realistic and compassionate struggle for responsibility and community in the face of sin – in 'us' as well as in 'them'. Again, there are many irresponsible demands for 'responsibility' amongst workers and trade unions which prevent serious encounters with issues of power and justice in our society as it is today.

If, as Christians, we do no better than the slogan responses of

134

our neighbours and the people of our own sort (or class), then we are pretty clearly not open to God in his work and are in grave danger of being, in practice, atheists. I am sure that this is a very serious challenge which God presents to us, in accordance with the pattern of the 'controversy' which he has always had with his people (see, for example, Micah 6.2). But we must be clear, from the biblical Christian tradition, that God never confronts us with judgment and challenge without at the same time, and through the very judgment, offering us ways of forgiveness and means of responding in creativity and hope.

As a way forward, therefore, we are bound to add to the simplicity that 'God is in reality' the simplicity of 'Jesus Christ, the same yesterday, and today, and for ever' (Hebrews 13.8).

In this phrase, 'yesterday' points to what Jesus has been presented and proclaimed to be and invites us to draw fearlessly on the whole New Testament and early church tradition. Of course this tradition will and must be questioned, but since it is a living tradition stemming from a living faith, the very questioning is to do with its continually coming alive. 'Today' refers to what Jesus is found to be by so many Christians in so many places and in so many circumstances in our present world. It includes the witness and delivery (however feeble and fluctuating) of our faith. It reminds us that 'being a Christian' is a matter of relying on God's giving of himself 'in Christ' now, and that we cannot escape either the challenge or the opportunity of reaffirming our own testimony and risking our own obedience and experience. 'And for ever' (Greek: *eis tous aionas*, to the ages): both the presentation of Jesus and the finding out about him will go on to the very end. So having to rethink and rediscover about Jesus Christ and his significance is not a contradiction of his livingness but the very expression of it. For he points to the God who is in reality and who is God indeed. And the Godness of God is infinite – so there is always more to be learnt of him and from him, and sometimes the 'more' may seem to destroy some of what we thought we knew. Sometimes we are to be led into this 'more' of God through the real newness in history. Thus we may find ourselves bewildered at times, but newness and expansion in our understanding of Christ

135

is what is offered to us. He is not 'our' Christ. He is God's Christ and we have no monopoly on the correct understanding of him.

Jesus Christ is both the basis of our faith and our invitation to discipleship and pilgrimage. He who is 'the same' is the living Christ who with the Father and the Spirit is the oneness of the Holy and the Living Trinity. So the resources are infinite and quite capable of coping with all history and with all of us.

Another well-known sentence later in the chapter leads to a further simplicity: 'For here we have no continuing city but we seek one to come' (Hebrews 13.14). The Greek says: 'For here we do not have a *menousan* city but we seek the *mellousan* one'; there is almost certainly some sort of pun here which might be roughly rendered: 'We do not possess an *abiding* city; we seek an *arriving* one.' The resources of yesterday and today are there for the future and only for that future which is God's future. We have to do with 'the once and future king'.

Here, in the face of all the complexities, we have the fundamental simplicity of the kingdom. It is God's. It has come in Jesus Christ ('the same yesterday and today'), so it will come in God's time and place (i.e. 'at the end of the ages' and 'throughout each and every age' – as long as they last). Our job is to respond to God through Jesus in the Holy Spirit now.

This involves taking up once again whatever we have so far found to be the resources of the Christian tradition. On that basis we are called to face up to what is going on now. And in and through those resources we are to look for judgment, newness and endurance. One thing is clear. We cannot go on as we are and we should not go on as we are. To do this would be to practise atheism. Whatever potential decisions we take about 'abiding' and 'keeping things going' must be tempered by our overall concern with 'arriving' and being moved to God's future and contributing to it.

If what we call Christian belonging bogs us down and closes us in against contemporary realities, then it is idolatry. This is the perennial sin of God's people. And as the Bible and the Christian tradition show, God, who is the living God known through Jesus Christ in the Spirit, is constantly troubling his people to move from their idolatrous abiding to a living, hopeful, sustaining and suffering arriving.

Faithfulness to the God who is in reality and who is as he is in the Jesus Christ who is the same yesterday, today and for ever demands that we should not go on as we are. We seek the city that is to come.

But what does that mean, in reality?

Since God is in reality, he means us to respond to and make something of the practicalities, the problems, and the uncertainties of our dailiness. He is certainly not an 'if only' God. ('If only conditions were different, then we could serve ...') Our pilgrimage and our ministry can go on from where we now are. The 'going on' will involve readiness for unexpectedness, for newness and for loss. There will be opportunities of finding out what we can do, and constraints of facing up to what we cannot do and what we can do without. So we are to respond to the practicalities but not to be dominated or defined by them.

This means that we must expect and organize to make short-term and medium-term plans and projects. We should therefore build up a discipline (with the help of others) for making such plans, carrying them out, monitoring them and so changing them or dropping them. This is life and this is pilgrimage. The pattern, the promise and the fulfilment is God's. The simplicity of the kingdom offers us a picture and a promise, not a blueprint. We are called to be fellow workers with God.

First, this means that the work is with God, so that the provisionalities are ours, while the pattern and the fulfilment is his. Secondly, however, we are fellow workers. There are real and worthwhile things to plan, do and attempt – out of obedience and as offerings (as we shall see when we come to consider worship). Our concern is with obedience and offering, not with the success or failure of our service of God and our calling as Christians. Success and failure are simply secondary working notions to be applied to our monitoring and replanning and the continuing or dropping of enterprises undertaken. That is to say that success and failure are criteria notions to be applied to our short-term and medium-term plans and projects. They are neither permanent nor primary. *That* is God in process, the living God, the kingdom of God and his Christ. Nothing else is primary and permanent. We shall all certainly die and all our churches will come to be ruins. We have no abiding city. We have only and always an arriving one. So ministry and spirituality require that we be severely practical, continually rethinking and replanning. I would suggest that various spiritualities could and should contribute to this, and it is these that I shall now go on to explore.

1. *The spirituality of the aporia point*. I take the word aporia from Plato's account of Socrates' method. Socrates' famous 'irony' was developed by his questioning through which he brought his companion to that form of self-knowledge which involves facing what you do not know. To lose one's familiar and taken-for-granted assurances is to be ready for moving on along the path of true knowledge and creative newness. Aporia is the state of not having a path (*poros*) obviously before you – perhaps a Greek term for 'being in the wildnerness'?

We have to consider the *cost* of newness and the bewilderment of pilgrimage and purpose pursued through change. Just how many thoughtful doctors and others deeply concerned with health care are reaching their 'aporia point'? Both the routines and the structures which were developed for caring and for promoting health are somehow not working – or worse. So what is the way forward? In this crisis one's professional identity and even one's personal commitment seems to be dissolving. It is very painful and bewildering. But the facts are as they are, and so openness to reality and staying with one's original commitment leaves one at an aporia point.

Concerned people in many institutions and walks of life find themselves in similar conditions. One might think of prison administrators, prison officers and all those caught up in our criminal justice system. And surely this reflects also the condition of many Christian ministers and disciples.

The vital point is this. The strong Christian, the man or woman of strong and living faith, is the one who receives the grace of God *to stay at the aporia point*. Life, my discipleship, our common service, the daily practicalities and realities together with the complexities of their context have brought me or us to this point of aporia. We are uncertain. There is the confusion of not knowing: of not knowing what to do (parish strategy and tactics), of not knowing what to say (sermon), of not even knowing what to believe ('Lord, I believe, help thou mine unbelief'). God is in reality and *this* is our reality. So here we stay until we spot newness or are given newness.

Further, the God who is in reality is the God who is as he is in Jesus. Therefore we are quite clear that newness, creativity, salvation come at a cost. Not to know where you are or where you are going or where you ought to go can be exciting, exhilarating and opening up. At times it can be, and certainly will be, hell: painfully costly; well-nigh crucifying. But here you/we are – at this aporia point, and we must not go back. We must stay until God moves us on. Again and again it is an aporia point which is *the* place of faith, of obedience, of witness and mission. We must therefore develop a spirituality of the aporia point for effective ministry.

2. *The spirituality of collaboration*. No *one* (person on his or her own) is 'sufficient for these things'.

This is an axiom of spirituality anyway. All is *of grace* and God's service is perfect freedom. It is through our dependence that we are offered a freedom in however adverse circumstances. Therefore we have a chance to be free from megalomania and the 'it all depends on me and there is far too much to do' syndrome. This syndrome has to be bust up whether it is self-induced, induced by the community or congregation, or collusively produced. One most significant expression of a lively spirituality is cutting down on one's commitments and expectations.

Collaboration is a necessity in our complex world because as individuals in a particular role (or set or roles) we cannot possibly have the requisite knowledge or the necessary first-hand sensitivities to and experiences of what is going on. So we must live, think and respond with and through others.

We cannot possibly make all the necessary difficult judgments on our own. Creative living and creative activity require the maintaining of difficult balances between so many tensions and conflicting (as well as unclear) demands. So we need the support and criticism of others as we work our own way through necessary decisions and difficult balancing acts. Otherwise we become simplistic and fall for the idolatry of the simple solution (being simple with the simplicity which sustains openness does not produce 'simple-mindedness' or childishness – the fanatic is not the man of faith but the child of fear) or because we do not have sufficient support from others, the tensions and the tension-maintaining easily slide from promoting stimulating stress into producing debilitating strain.

And in any case, while discipleship must often involve loneliness and living on inner resources we are not called as Christians simply to suffer on our own.

Therefore we must develop a spirituality of collaboration which has to be both a spirituality that can cope with collaboration and spirituality which grows out of collaboration.

However, the way to this does not lie through over-romantic expectations of a congregation as *koinonia* or fellowship. Rather each of us has, according to our circumstances and temperaments, to work out clear strategies and practice for working at keeping 'maintenance congregations' going; developing pilgrim groups and finding a sustaining community which operates as the 'church for me'. All this is part of developing a spirituality of collaboration for sustaining the spirituality of the aporia point.

3. *The spirituality of God*. It might seem absurd to make this a separate 'spirituality', for surely *all* spirituality is about God.

This is, of course, so. But I believe that we do not grapple sufficiently in a direct way with the issue of 'God'. It is all very well to say that God is in reality, but how can we 'desloganize' him?

This means that each of us has to develop persistent ways in which we pursue the risky and fearful business of exploring our answers to the questions 'What do *I* mean by "God"?' and 'What does "God" mean to me?' We have to reflect prayerfully and openly about the (partly describable) foci or loci of the experience and experiences when God comes down to *my* earth. (If, for example, God may be referred to as 'transcendence in the midst', then what are the examples of 'the midst' in which I experience,

140

glimpse, seek after, feel after, have the impression that I have to do with, transcendence?) I touch on this subject and stumblingly make a few fairly futile and inadequate attempts to tackle it because I think that it is inescapable – not because I find it at all 'handlable'.

This God is not only *at* the aporia point, he also *is* an aporia point. Knowing him and not knowing him seem very much the same thing: *and yet* there is an awareness, a beckoning, a reaching out to that which (he who) is a response. As soon as I attend to myself attending to God I have, of course, 'lost God'; *nevertheless* there is an attending and a being found and a being obliged to be still of which one has some memory, some impression, and for which one has some irremovable longing. Of course it might well all be imagination, fantasy and romance, but there is a hint, a promise and an enticement of glory, even if, as soon as one becomes self-conscious about it, 'the glory' is always around the corner ('My face thou cannot see . . .'). So God is the presence remembered in absence, the one whom I will know. God is the God of all the fathers (and the mothers!) of faith and the God of Jesus whom I seek because he has sought me and beckons me. It is God whom I must dare to claim, in some sense, to 'know' because our corporate knowledge and experience as Christians and in the tradition assures us that God indeed knows me.

Perhaps all this sounded like nonsense when it was said and reads even more like nonsense now. Yet it is necessary to develop this (largely and usually hidden) discipline, search and spirituality which is directly about God because it is the sole justification and point of all that we do or attempt to do. God is what we long for (the value of all values which is not valuable but just is). God is what we look for, the fulfilment of our hearts' desire which is quite beyond all we could possibly desire. God is what we expect to 'come out of it all', to be the consummation of it all, the final resting place who is perfect peace, communion and joy. There is no other purpose than God and there is no purpose to God. He is – God.

For glimpses and fleeting foci or loci of him we may contemplate all we know of love – and then more, far more. We may cherish all we know of beauty – wherever we glimpse it – in the countryside, in music, in the glimpsed moment, in the faces of people; and God is more, far more. We may recall every moment of joy and dwell with the thought that God is more, far more. We have been given a pointer when we knew and felt 'This is it!'; when we have briefly wondered why 'this' should not go on for ever. We have a hint when we catch ourselves so enjoying something that we say 'I do not need to do more than catch myself enjoying this and then forget myself'.

All this is both on the way to God and a being in touch with God (a being touched by God). So God is all peace – and more. And, in a derived way and dependent on all that I have tried to say, God is all purpose – and more. When something worthwhile is achieved, when there is a fitting together of things, when there is a sense, and especially a shared sense, of 'bringing it off', we are in touch with and pointed towards God.

God is thus love, beauty, joy, purpose and peace. And when 'it' is all about – and what we are all about is – God. This total subjection of everything to God in no way diminishes us or everything else. Rather it gives demands and promises *glory* to us and through everything else. For God invites us, entices us, provokes us and waits for us to share himself. And so in our life, pilgrimage and ministry now he is inviting us to share in discovery, developing and showing partial and temporary outcomes of and preprations for *his* love, beauty, joy, purpose and peace.

Finally, note that, being God, he is both independent of everything else and involved in everything else. This is, perhaps, the crux of 'the spirituality of God', for it invites us to practise an attachment and a detachment. He is to be sought and served in the busyness of maintaining things and institutions and in the struggles with all our problems. This is the way of our service of God and of our ministry, in and through all these things. But also (and also) he is God, despite all these things, over against all these things, relativizing all these things, beyond all these things and quite independently of all these things. Unless we can develop our own practice of this twofold spirituality of dynamic tension we shall be

142

lost in idolatry (e.g. of maintaining institutions at all costs or of worshipping problem-solving) and our lives and our ministries will be full of mere (and increasingly joyless) reaction. Therefore, to be added to and sought through the spirituality of the aporia point and the spirituality of collaboration is the spirituality of God.

4. *The spirituality of worship*. The continuing and corporate practice of worship is quite central to any ministry and discipline and a central source from which we are to draw both criteria for judging our actions, responses and plans and our sense of vision and direction.

Worship is the conscious and corporate attempt to focus on and recognize the 'Godness of God' as we are called to know him through and in the name of Jesus Christ. In the practice and conduct of worship the stories told and the forms and the language used have to resonate with the tradition and to resonate with now.

I fancy that we should be clear that there is no general formula (to be worked out, e.g., by a liturgical commission) which will either restore 'the beauty of the liturgy', 'the centrality of the Book of Common Prayer', 'the splendour of the Authorized Version' or will guarantee relevance. Authenticity, beauty and relevance have all to be sought by us locally and congregationally with whatever help (or hindrance) we can get from 'the experts'. The worship of wayfaring men and women has three strands to it. It is a *response* to what has been heard, found and done through our membership of the church and our Christian discipleship. Every worshipper must bring his or her own active and personal component to worship. 'Being in the pew' is an *active* affair. It is a *remembering* – hence the service being shaped around biblical and traditional material. There is a tradition and core of revelation which must be responsibly recalled, and we must not be afraid of retaining what strikes us as strange or what cannot immediately be assimilated or made something of. And it is a *search* for God now, for what is to be done now and to be looked forward to now.

Once again, as with aporia, there can be no going back to nostalgically recollected (and idealized!) patterns of worship. We have to stay where we are, discover the presence in our worship and then go on. So we must be quite clear about the central importance in our ministry of the conduct of worship. In practice we have to work to maintain worship, we have also to struggle to improve worship, and we have to develop or restore a calmness in the sheer acceptance of worship in whatever form we have it. Worship does not depend on 'getting the rite right'.

It is, I believe, from the steady maintenance of and focussing on worship that we shall chiefly discover the distinctive contributions which we ought to bring as Christians to our problems and duties as citizens. For worship focusses our attention on true 'worship-fulness' and on the supreme criterion of human worth, which is that everything should be moved in the direction of being an offering worthy of the love of God and capable of promoting the sharing of and response to that love in the relationships between human beings.

Thus 'offerability' becomes a central criterion of moral worth and social significance. And 'sin' is to be understood as all that distorts, prevents and fights against such 'offerability'. It is from our worship, therefore, that we are to draw our developed understanding of what it is to sin and of the judgments we ought to receive on our own conduct and attitudes. It is then, as informed and forgiven sinners, that we can convey and fight for the judgments which ought to be made about so much public and general wickedness, selfishness and triviality. We ought to be able to build up out of our worship a growing understanding of what *changes* ought to be sought now and for the immediately coming years; we should also spot what evils should be *mitigated*; and we should build up a community of response to those things which have to be *endured*. A worshipful way of life is full of purpose, hope and joy even under conditions of great unsatisfactoriness (say, a falling standard of living and great social and political uncertainty).

The blending of worship into our spirituality, our ministry and our way of life is, I fancy, quite central to lively discipleship and effective human living and so to creative Christian witness and service.

144

5. *The spirituality of salvation.* Of course, all these 'spiritualities' interlock. I am simply distinguishing them for the sake of exposition and emphasis. And the final emphasis I want briefly to mention is to do with the practice of the knowledge that the gospel is about salvation and not about solutions.

The gospel is the good news about God – that is the Redeemer and Saviour who promises a fulfilment totally worthy of him and unbelievably satisfying for us which is established 'in the end', in God's own time and place, i.e. in God's being and eternity. What we are now dealing with are foretastes and 'down-payments' of the kingdom.

Thus all solutions and resolutions of all the problems and opportunities which face us individually, corporately, nationally or universally are temporary, partial and provisional. Our search for ways forward and for positive responses in the short and medium term is not negated by failure and bafflement, by things going wrong and by encountering barriers which confront us with our own powerlessness. All planning for and striving for good ends is part of our required response to the goodness of God and his invitation to be part of his creative and redeeming work. Our part is to seek and to contribute. It is his part to judge, redeem and fulfil. So we can and should approach our tasks in society with an open-eyed realism about the effects of sin and the presence of sometimes devastating limitations. All this does not turn us aside from attempts at service and at change which should be made and from the persistent pursuit of ideals which we know ought to be aimed at.

For example, a developed 'spirituality of salvation' should enable us in the political sphere to be both realistic about the failures that have developed in the 1940s conception of the Welfare State while at the same time not lose the political will to seek to care for people in need, to make health care, unemployment support and so on available to those in need and to try for device after device to extend the 'social security' that is available to all citizens. Or again, the way to practical and effective applications of 'small is beautiful' is as difficult as is the way of enabling our big institutions to function better. But, believing as we do in a God who cares for all, we must not cease to look for ways of deepening the caring of society and of relationships in society. Our knowledge of salvation and of the Saviour should set us free to renew our social, political and human searches again and again and not to be dominated either by false expectations (e.g. of political systems) or by inhuman cynicism (e.g. about what you can expect of people).

The message of salvation, which transcends all solutions and all failures to find solutions, gives us renewed hope and purpose as we face failures, recognize limits and seek repeatedly to renew projects and programmes pursuing short- and medium-term aims in our society. And, perhaps most importantly of all, seeing that the gospel of salvation is focussed in and through Jesus, this message and its appropriate spirituality of response enables us to see that we have hope and purpose, and can be part of offering hope and purpose to others, in the bearing of cost and the enduring of suffering.

The central symbols of cross and resurrection have to mark our lives and inform our daily living, social and political, as well as personal and individual. There is no hopeful way forward and no sustaining purpose and joy to be found in human living if we cannot take into account, and share in, what has to be borne and what has to be suffered. Pain, grief, loss and despair are part of human living and do not negate the possibilities and promises of salvation. The transfigured Christ who gave an anticipatory glimpse of the glorified Christ is the disfigured and the crucified Christ. All this is not 'high doctrine' and pious rhetoric. It points to and is part of the pattern of salvation and we must not want to be exempted from it. Indeed, what realistic hope we can be part of if God gives us grace to go this way.

The spirituality of salvation is shaped by experience of the resources of God that go beyond and from time to time contradict everything that we experience or invest in. It may be that it is just when all solutions are out of our grasp that we may know ourselves to be within the scope of God's salvation. Such knowledge returns us in practice to the struggles, the joys, the celebrations and the pains of aporia, of collaboration, of the search for God which is itself response to God, and of the practice and pursuit of worship.

As a conclusion, I cannot do better than to quote a passage from the New Testament which is also a reminder of apparent limitations in response to the gospel:

'For we preach not ourselves but Christ Jesus the Lord: and ourselves your servant for Jesus' sake. For God, who commanded the light to shine out of darkness, hath shined in our hearts to give the light of the knowledge of the glory of God in the face of Jesus Christ.' That is, we are called to serve the purpose of Almighty God in and for creation in our ministry and spirituality as it is related to 'all who have faces' – to men and women as persons who are meant to be related to the glory of God.

'But we have this treasure in earthen vessels, that the excellency of the power may be of God and not of us.'

The spirituality of God has to be practised in relation to, and to overflow into, everything. *That* is what our ministry is about. And if that awesome fact makes us say 'God help us', we may reflect: 'Mais c'est son métier.' That is precisely what God is about in Jesus. He helps and he saves.